THE PROSPERITY doHow®

INSPIRING GROWTH EMPOWERING LIVES

DINAKAR MURTHY KRISHNA

ISBN 979-8-89446-631-6

Contents

Foreword

I have known Dinakar since he started his career at Bosch in 1986 by joining my team at MICO—later Bosch Ltd. He was then an aspiring and smart engineer fresh out of college. His career has grown in leaps and bounds from a manufacturing process engineer, product division head, and a technical chief of one of the major Bosch plants. I recall the time and effort he spent on the shop floor in a practice called "Do it Right" (DIR). This involved discussing with cross-functional team members at Gemba and coming up with solutions to various problems. Experiences like this helped him grow his knowledge both technically and managerially. As his career blossomed, he gathered more learning and experiences both in India and abroad, which helped bring him to the level he has now reached as a successful entrepreneur.

He has now applied his writing talent in this book, wherein he has shared the experiences he has gained along with the know-how/concepts and tools he has pioneered and developed to support the manufacturing industry at large for improvement. The guiding principles and concepts developed are based on sound, time-tested principles, e.g., PDCA, lean, problem-solving, etc. The book, with its three basic practices of CORE, SUSTAIN and ADVANCE, covers a broad array of topics—from mindset and culture, people aspects, leadership, goal setting, strategy development, sales and operations, the importance of metrics and many more. In addition, he has researched our ancient traditions and principles and adapted them to suit his purpose of diagnosing the organisation's health.

The book uses an easy conversational style between the author and various persons, covering diverse organisational roles. This has the benefit of easy reading and assimilation of the concepts. These concepts are time-tested by Dinakar in the various consultancy projects executed by him to a wide variety of companies and organisations in the past eleven years. The impact has been significant, and each of the organisations has experienced excellent improvements.

Excellence is a tough journey for any organisation. Using the concepts and tools explained in this book can be of immense help for the reader and the organisation when they start their excellence journey. Thus, this book is a great help to all those who would like to make improvements in their organisations and work to achieve excellence.

K. G. Shashidhar

Retired Business Head,

MICO Bosch Bangalore.

Foreword

In the VUCA world of business, change is the only constant. Businesses seeking to excel in their operations must continuously evolve and adapt to better themselves on an ongoing basis. This necessitates a consequential change in the ecosystem in which the business operates. In a fiercely competitive environment, continuous adaptation is crucial; without it, success is not guaranteed. Even in less competitive businesses, continuous adaptation remains essential. The operating ecosystem must be tweaked as often as needed to pursue excellence.

Dinakar, whom I have known since he started his career at MICO, highlights the need for such transformation in every business in this book. He uses the analogy of how an eagle naturally transforms as it ages, shedding its feathers and moving from its current status quo to a new one, thus stepping out of its comfort zone into an unknown zone where it finds a new level of comfort. The transformation journey required for any organisation is explained through various elements as part of a holistic and Socratic learning approach called the doHow® approach, which he has developed based on his practical experience in various organisations during his chequered career.

The nuances involved in various organisational functions such as Sales, Design, Production Planning, Purchase, Logistics, etc., are explained through interactions and exchange of information with fictitious characters, in which the various elements of management covered in the doHow® approach are explained and this facilitates easy understanding as several practical situations are discussed in these interactions.

While every element of management is important, and each has been explained excellently, some stand out. Let us consider Time Management, for example. While it is customary to include elements of "importance" and "urgency" (both being "low" or "high") in a four-quadrant model, which is the standard approach, the author adds another two elements, namely, "routine" and "one-time", and converts this into an eight-quadrant model to explain the nuances involved in practising time management effectively.

Another aspect that stands out is the area related to "Mindset and Culture", which is extremely important in the aspect of Transformation through the use of both theories based on scientific research (readiness potential) and practice involving actual practical and real-life examples. The elements of true "Leadership" in contrast to "Management" have also been brought out very well, from being a "manager" or a "leader" to becoming a "leader manager", using the various levels of delegation.

Conversion of the Vision and Mission of an organisation into the practical approach of deployment of the strategy to achieve the goals by appropriately tracking the various KPIs by having clarity on the process as well as the outcome of the process has also been very well brought out in the book. The concept of Stakeholder Management in a holistic manner, including all external and internal stakeholders, has been described very well, and it is often not a very strong area in many organisations, and provides good learning. Another critical point is that of Problem Solving, which is also an important part of every business, and this has been addressed extremely well in the book.

Lastly, the book also carries a practical application of this holistic learning approach of doHow® by taking us through an actual case study, which has been given as a success story, wherein a doHow® Coach guides the people in the organisation on the application of the various elements of the doHow® approach and the transformation from a silo type of operation to a successful team approach is perceived by the participants themselves. This magical transformation takes the organisation to very great heights.

I had the privilege of going through the entire book and had a déjà vu experience, as several points in the case studies are real-life examples and I could relate it to similar experiences during my professional career. Therefore, I find the book to be extremely practical in nature. This book would be extremely useful for budding managers in any organisation and would act as a guiding torch for the person.

Readers would benefit enormously from this book.

I would like to congratulate Dinakar on this wonderful initiative to write a book of this nature by bringing out various learnings from his professional career.

M C Ramakrishnan

Retired Quality Head,

MICO Bosch, Bangalore

Acknowledgements

This book would never have been possible without the blessings and guidance of the divine power I call the 'Central Energy Source'— CES for short. I am profoundly grateful to CES for shaping my life journey with its many ups and downs, which have provided me with invaluable opportunities to explore, experiment, and learn. As the saying goes, the ultimate realisation is to do our best within our circle of influence and leave the rest to CES. I am thankful to CES for allowing me to internalise this wisdom throughout my journey so far and for the path ahead.

My deepest gratitude goes to my mother, Saroja K Murthy. Her determination to ensure that my younger brother, sister, and I were well-settled after the passing of my father when I was just eleven years old, and my sister only three has been a source of immense strength. I dedicate this book to my mother, whose resilience is a key attribute I have inherited from her.

I am also thankful to my subordinates, peers, and superiors from my corporate career in India, Brazil, and Germany. They have pushed me in ways they might not even realise, enabling me to continually learn and evolve. The foundation of "The Prosperity doHow®" lies in the experiential learning from my corporate career. The final refinement of these ideas came through my clients, who graciously provided me with opportunities to research, explore, experiment, and learn. I am extremely grateful to them for allowing me to introduce and implement many concepts, such as Prosperity Chakras, Maturity Scale, Process Excellence, Role

Description, Regular Reporting, One-on-one Dialogue, and more, as explained in the following chapters.

Thinking of possible solutions to my clients' challenges comes naturally to me—thanks to CES and everyone who has helped shape me. However, it's essential to bounce off these thoughts to gain different perspectives and create robust solutions. I am incredibly thankful to my spouse, Dr Usha Dinakar, who has always been my go-to person for this. I am also extremely grateful to my daughter, Madhuri Dinakar, who has sparked new ideas in me, especially when I was stuck. I extend my heartfelt thanks to my colleagues, Sagar Moudgal and Vivek Palsule, who have not only stood by me in delivering value to our clients but have also been inspired and excited by the concepts I developed.

Finally, I want to thank all my well-wishers for their support and encouragement in writing this book, with a special thanks to both Mr K G Shashidhar, my first boss and mentor, and to Mr M C Ramakrishnan, another mentor for writing a foreword for my book.

Thank you all from the bottom of my heart.

Preface

During the 1990s, many top executives at Bosch would mock Indian vendors, including Bosch in India, for initially supplying good samples on time but then delivering defective products and failing to meet delivery commitments. As an Indian who became the first foreigner to serve as an executive assistant to the board of management, I found this deeply uncomfortable. My own experience of supplying high-precision components with zero defects, from India to Japan and Brazil to Germany, using very old machines, made me challenge these negative sentiments at Bosch. This prompted me to embark on a journey to uncover the secret to consistently delivering high-quality, precise products on time and in full.

I believed that the key to the renowned German Engineering and Japanese Precision, beyond innovative product development, was the consistent delivery of good quality on time and in full, or simply put, excellence in execution. This belief was reinforced during my mentoring of many companies since leaving my corporate career in 2013. I observed that only those companies that focused on this consistency and developed practices to ensure they have been consistently growing beyond their sectoral average year after year.

While systems were the visible differentiators in these companies, it became clear to me that the true differentiators were people, mindset, and culture. I realised the importance of creating the right mindset and culture to develop systems that enable excellence in execution. This realisation led me to experiment with various methods for changing mindsets and culture, resulting in the creation of doHow®, a Socratic Learning Methodology, which I now use in my mentoring assignments.

I decided to write this book, 'The Prosperity doHow®,' based on my experiences in transforming the mindset and culture of many aspiring individuals to achieve excellence in execution, the path to prosperity. I wanted to share my understanding of the keys to prosperity, that I discovered, so more people beyond my direct clients could benefit and prosper.

Another motivation for writing this book was the paradoxical situation in micro, small, and medium enterprises. These companies, which need exceptionally skilled people to navigate daily challenges amid high uncertainty, often end up with mediocre employees. Conversely, large and multinational companies, which could manage with average employees to execute established systems, attract exceptional talent due to their financial power. However, my experience working closely with many so-called 'mediocre' employees in smaller enterprises revealed that they are, in fact, exceptional individuals with great aspirations, hindered only by lack of exposure. On the other hand, exceptional people in large companies often resort to mediocrity due to compliance pressures and need something to reignite their spark and unleash their potential.

I hope this book will provide insights and inspiration to consistently deliver high-quality products on time, unlocking the path to prosperity for many more people and organisations.

dinakarmurthy.com

businessdohow.com

dinakar@businessdohow.com

Introduction

In the complex and ever-evolving landscape of modern business, achieving and sustaining prosperity demands more than just traditional management techniques. The Prosperity doHow®, a book I wrote based on my experiences in iteratively developing doHow®, a Socratic Learning Methodology, integrates timeless principles with innovative, yet simple, practices. This comprehensive guide is designed to equip leaders, managers, and organisations with the tools necessary for navigating their journey towards excellence.

The Prosperity doHow® is structured around three foundational ideas: CORE, SUSTAIN, and ADVANCE, each representing a vital aspect of business operations and growth, explained in the next chapter.

CORE: The Bedrock of Excellence is an acronym for Common Understanding, Ongoing Pledge, Regular Audit, and Endless Retraining. It is grounded in the Deming Cycle (Plan-Do-Check-Act) and serves as the foundation for aligning the organisation towards common goals. CORE practices emphasise the importance of routine and discipline, much like the strategic time-outs in team sports that recalibrate focus and strategy.

SUSTAIN: Ensuring Consistency and Delivery with another crucial acronym, which stands for Surge Common Understanding, Strategy Development and Detailing, Articulate Execution Plan with Buffer, Implement with Monitoring and Steering, and Natural

Problem Solving and Dialogue. It mirrors the Policy Deployment or Hoshin Kanri cycle.

Through SUSTAIN, organisations can create a closed-loop system that continuously learns and improves, ensuring that strategic initiatives are effectively implemented and sustained.

ADVANCE: Driving Growth and Evolution represents the phases necessary for organisational growth and transformation. It includes Assess Old Status Quo, Detailed Goal Setting, Vanquish Resistance, Address Confusion, Nurture Learning, Consolidate Learning, and Establish New Status Quo.

ADVANCE ensures that organisations are not just maintaining their current state but are continuously evolving and improving.

Welcome to an exciting journey where the enablers of prosperity are unveiled, driving an excellence revolution that promises to significantly enhance the quality of life for all. Imagine a world where every aspect of business aligns seamlessly, working together to create harmony, efficiency, and unprecedented success, as an effect of just one champion initiating a transformation inspired by this book. This is the vision of The Prosperity doHow®, that blends timeless principles with simple practices to elevate organisations to new heights by inspiring people to leverage the CORE, SUSTAIN, and ADVANCE.

Every topic necessary for The Prosperity doHow® is explained in the chapters that follow as a conversation between me and a fictional character, based on real people known to me. The final chapter before the conclusion contains a success story, again with fictional characters based on real people known to me.

You are invited to explore The Prosperity doHow® to unleash the power of your will in pursuit of excellence by understanding, focusing, and leveraging the CORE, SUSTAIN, and ADVANCE to your advantage. The three simple questions at the end of each chapter as 'Homework' are intended to actually get going, apart from just getting mentally inspired. Reading the book completely, either in one go or by taking pauses, for an overview before reading those chapters, which may be your weakest links for generating actionable insights for releasing your hidden potential, is recommended.

Core, Sustain and Advance

During my days as a teen, the only entertainment was reading books. I loved reading books such as Airport, Hotel, Wheels, The Final Diagnosis, and The Money Changers written by Arthur Hailey, which basically described the inside stories of the different business verticals. The book 'In Search of Excellence' by Tom Peters and Robert H. Waterman Jr. inspired me and, in a way, paved the path to my lifelong journey of discovering excellence. The Machine That Changed the World, written by James P. Womack, Daniel T. Jones, and Daniel Roos, introduced me to the world of Lean. Last but not least, I was introduced to the Theory of Constraints, ToC for short, with the book The Goal written by Eliyahu M. Goldratt. I was inspired both by Lean and ToC, and both have moulded the way I perceive, think, decide, and act during my entire life as I progressed in my corporate career before embarking on an entrepreneurship journey of mentoring, coaching, and consulting.

After almost 40 years of living and experiencing Lean and ToC, I introduce three basic practices of exceptional leaders and world-class companies – CORE, SUSTAIN, and ADVANCE.

CORE, an acronym I created for **C**ommon Understanding, **O**ngoing Pledge, **R**egular Audit, and **E**ndless Retraining, is based on the Deming Cycle or the Plan-Do-Check-Act Cycle. CORE is the foundation for getting everyone on the same page with a common understanding, reinforcing the purpose and the rules of the game with a daily pledge to achieve outstanding outcomes, daily audit followed by immediate containment and correction to ensure adherence to the rules of the game and weekly endless retraining based on the audit outcomes for continual learning and improvement.

Reflecting on my own experiences, I have found that periodically contemplating the ideal state, preferably at least once a quarter, facilitates the prompt implementation of new insights, propelling us towards a continuous journey of improvement. Beyond individual awareness of the ideal state, fostering a collective common understanding among the entire team regarding both the ideal state and the current reality is paramount for determining the ideal-reality gap. This practice aligns with the planning or standardising phase of the Deming Excellence Plan-Do-Check-Act cycle.

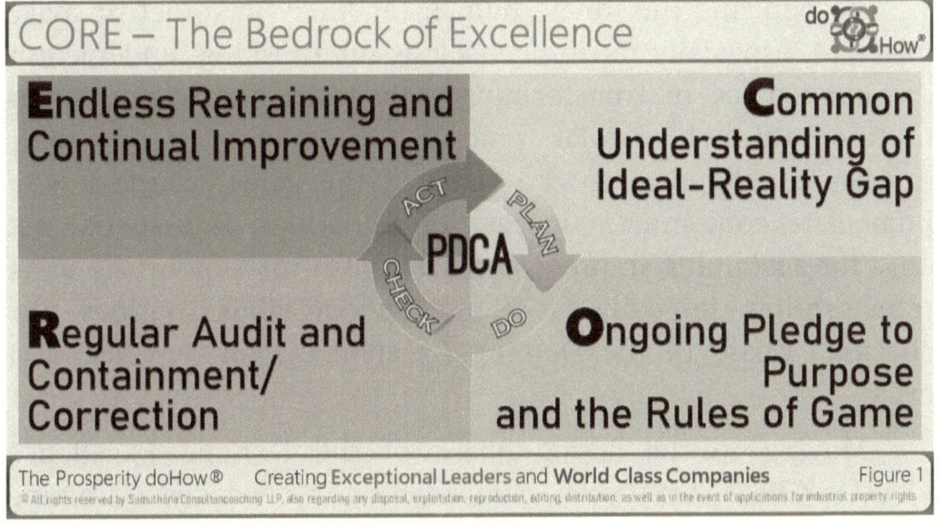

The documented outcome of the common understanding is the mission, vision, and values. The mission of a business is a clear and compelling statement that defines its purpose or the sole reason for its existence as an entity, guides its actions, and communicates its unique value to employees, customers, and stakeholders. An aspirational vision of a company is a forward-looking statement that outlines its long-term goals and dreams, inspiring and motivating stakeholders by painting a picture of a desirable future it strives to achieve. The values of a business are the core principles and beliefs that guide its behaviours, decisions, and actions, shaping its culture and defining its ethical standards.

Once the gaps between the ideal and reality are identified, a common purpose for any manufacturing company emerges—to continually or perpetually bridge this gap, in addition to fulfilling its unique purpose. This purpose is guided by the company's values and boundaries, essentially forming the rules of the game. Drawing parallels to impactful routines from our school days, like morning prayers and proverbs, in a manufacturing setting, a daily pledge to the purpose and the rules of the game becomes a fundamental routine for excellence—the doing phase of the Deming Excellence Plan-Do-Check-Act cycle.

Recognising the innate human tendency to forget or make mistakes, especially during conscious multitasking, underscores the importance of transforming daily tasks into subconscious routines through regular practice. Conducting daily audits to ensure adherence to the rules of the game, coupled with immediate containment in case of deviations, is essential not only for sustaining improvements but also for supporting us in transforming the daily tasks into subconscious routines—the checking phase of the Deming Excellence Plan-Do-Check-Act cycle.

Moving to the acting phase of the Deming Excellence Plan-Do-Check-Act cycle, characterised by weekly retraining sessions on the purpose, ideal-reality gaps, rules of the game, audit outcomes, and systematic focused improvements based on the Pareto principle, enables internalisation of insights derived from the checking phase. This phase, crucial for learning and improvement, leads to updated policies, guidelines, processes, procedures, and instructions within the company.

CORE is just basic common sense, which, unfortunately, is forgotten in many struggling companies but is the foundation of all the world-class companies I have known. It is very much like what happens in team sports like cricket, soccer, basketball, etc., during the strategic time-out—a time to quickly speak of the CORE with the entire team. This simple practice is such a game-changer, as we all know. In world-class companies, CORE is integral to the day-to-day working and is practised without anyone really noticing. The awareness and importance of the CORE are necessary for diagnosing the situation and implementing remedial measures in organisations.

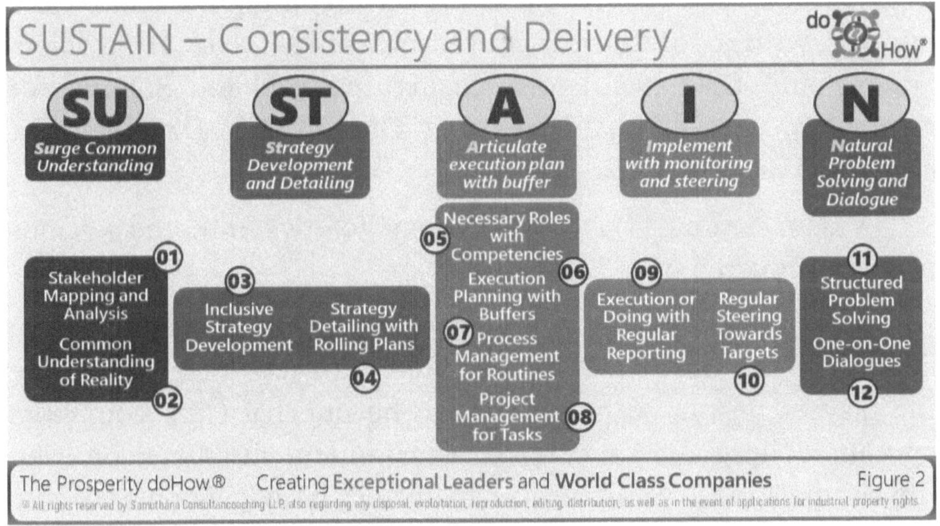

SUSTAIN, another acronym I created for **Su**rge Common Understanding, **St**rategy Development and Detailing, **A**rticulate Execution Plan with Buffer, **I**mplement with Monitoring and Steering, and **N**atural Problem Solving and Dialogue, is also the normal Policy Deployment or Hoshin Kanri cycle.

Surge common understanding comprises Stakeholder Mapping and Analysis for understanding the expectations, and Common Understanding of Reality for creating the baseline. Strategy Development and Detailing contains Inclusive Strategy Development with all the key players and Strategy Detailing with Rolling Plans for deploying the strategy through the assigned owners for key performance indicators. Articulate execution plan with buffer includes definition of Necessary Roles with Competencies for establishing the roles and responsibilities, Execution Planning with Buffers for aiming higher than targets to counter the unknown hurdles, Process Management for Routines for achieving consistency in established good practices and Project Management for Tasks with handover full kits for on spec, on time, on budget completion of projects. Implement, with monitoring and steering, encompasses Execution or Doing with Regular Reporting, especially for enabling the other team members, and Regular Steering Towards Targets for overcoming the confronted hurdles with coordinated countermeasures. Natural Problem Solving and Dialogue involve Structured Problem Solving for rational or system challenges and One-on-One Dialogues for emotional or people challenges.

Video gaming is a good analogy to dive into the various practices covered in SUSTAIN.

Stakeholder Mapping and Analysis: First things first, we need to figure out who's in the game with us. Stakeholders are the players on our team – they can be internal (like your boss or your colleagues) or external (customers, suppliers, or even the competition). Mapping and analysing them is like identifying who's in your squad. Knowing their needs and expectations will help us tailor our strategies to win together.

Common Understanding of Reality: Imagine playing a game where everyone has different rules in their heads. Chaos, right? The same goes for the workplace. We need to create a shared reality, a common understanding of what's happening. It's like agreeing on the rules before starting a game. That way, we are all on the same page and can work together effectively.

Inclusive Strategy Development: Now, let's get to the fun part – strategy! Instead of top-down decisions, involve everyone. The exceptionally well-informed future leaders are all about collaboration and diversity of ideas. So, gather input from various stakeholders to create strategies that resonate with everyone. This way, you'll get more buy-in and enthusiasm for the game plan.

Strategy Detailing with Rolling Plans: No more five-year plans that gather dust! We are all about adaptability. Break your strategy into bite-sized chunks with quarterly, monthly, weekly, and even daily rolling plans. Think of it like levelling up in a video game, moving you nearer to confronting the ultimate challenge.

Necessary Roles with Competencies: In any game, you have a diverse set of characters with unique abilities. In policy deployment, you need the right roles along with the right skills. For example:

Sales Executive (The Deal Closer): Connects with customers, persuades them to buy products, and ensures they have a seamless shopping experience.

Product/Service Designer (The Design Dynamo): Crafts and refines products or services, blending creativity with strategic insight to develop innovative solutions tailored to meet customer needs and business goals.

Product/Process Developer (The Production Architect): Responsible for developing and refining efficient processes and products, utilising strategic thinking and innovative approaches to optimise consistent production and delivery.

Purchaser (The Supply Sleuth): Hunts for the best deals on raw materials, negotiates with suppliers, and keeps costs in check.

Manufacturing Engineer (The Process Prodigy): Improves production processes, introduces new technologies, and boosts efficiency on the factory floor.

Production Planner (The Production Maestro): Plans manufacturing schedules, coordinates resources, and keeps the production line running smoothly.

Production Controller (The Workflow Wizard): Monitors production processes, identifies bottlenecks, and ensures everything runs like a well-oiled machine.

Maintenance Engineer (The Equipment Expert): Takes care of machinery and equipment, ensuring they're in good working order to keep production on track.

Production Supervisor (The Team Captain): Leads the production team, provides guidance, and ensures everyone's working safely and efficiently.

Quality Engineer (The Perfectionist): Inspects products, maintains quality standards, and collaborates with teams to fix any quality issues.

Accountant (The Numbers Ninja): Handles finances, tracks expenses, and ensures the company's financial health.

Execution Planning with Buffers: In gaming, we know that things rarely go as planned. So, include buffers in your execution plans. These are like extra lives in a game – they give you some breathing room when unexpected obstacles pop up. Trust us; you'll thank yourself later.

Process Management for Routines: Every organisation has routines – those everyday tasks that keep the ship sailing smoothly. Managing these efficiently is like mastering a combo move in a game. Use tools and processes to streamline these routines so you can focus on the real challenges.

Project Management for Tasks: Projects are your epic quests. Use project management tools to track tasks, set deadlines, and allocate resources. It's like having a quest log in your favourite RPG, helping you keep track of all the tasks and objectives.

Execution or Doing with Regular Reporting: It's time to get things done! Regular reporting is like saving your progress in a game – it shows you how far you've come and what's left to do. It's like sharing your progress and keeping your team and community updated on your achievements and challenges.

Regular Steering Towards Targets: To win the game, you need to steer towards your targets. Daily work management meetings are like quick strategy huddles. Weekly improvement meetings are your time to level up your skills. Monthly business reviews are your checkpoint for progress. Quarterly board meetings are the big boss battles.

Structured Problem Solving: When you encounter a tough level, you don't just keep hitting your head against the wall, right? You strategise and problem-solve. Apply the same principle at work. Use structured problem-solving techniques to overcome obstacles and reach your goals faster.

One-on-One Dialogues: Finally, don't forget the power of one-on-one dialogues. It's like having a heart-to-heart with your co-op partner in a multiplayer game. Use this time to bridge gaps, understand each other's perspectives, and fine-tune your strategies.

SUSTAIN practices, over and above the CORE, ensure consistency in delivering stakeholder expectations over time. These practices in world-class companies are internalised with an annual strategy and execution calendar culminating in a standard daily calendar for the organisation to work like a clock, continually learning and improving this closed-loop system with new insights that everyone is gathering during execution. Unfortunately, in many struggling companies, though performance management, some even with the balanced scorecard, is implemented, the end-to-end linkages for a seamless closed-loop process are basically missing. SUSTAIN is extremely important for sustainability.

ADVANCE, the last acronym necessary for growth, is a collection of **Assess Old Status Quo**, **Detailed Goal Setting**, **Vanquish Resistance**, **Address Confusion**, **Nurture Learning**, **Consolidate Learning**, and **Establish New Status Quo**, and can also be compared to the classical change management phases. These phases can also be seen in nature as an integral part of our evolution.

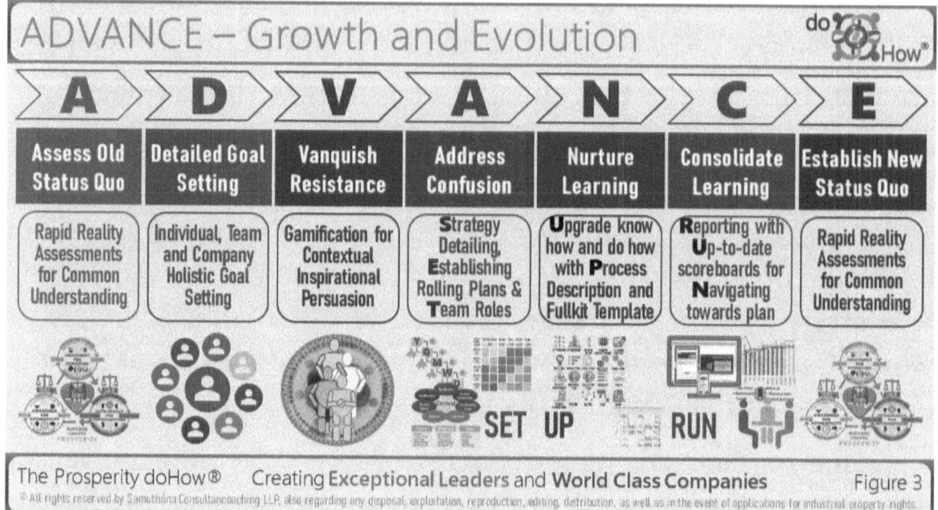

The evolution from a unicell organism to a multicell human being today has gone through multiple transformations over almost 4 billion years. Let us imagine we were in a different timescale, with maybe a million years corresponding to a day of our known timescale. Then, we would have witnessed evolution over maybe about ten years. Ten years is a good enough time to observe, analyse, and describe the phases of these transformations.

1. Ecosystems in nature normally maintain a certain level of stability over time, characterised by a balance of species interactions, resource availability, and environmental conditions.

2. Events that disrupt the existing equilibrium, such as changes in climate, geological events, or the emergence of new species (some predators), act as triggers for change in natural ecosystems.

3. Natural selection occurs to organisms resisting change, with some adapting to new conditions, surviving,

reproducing, and passing on their advantageous traits to future generations.

4. There is often confusion and chaos as the evolving species compete for resources and establish new relationships.

5. Biodiversity in nature provides a reservoir of genetic variation and innovation, allowing species to generate new traits and strategies in response to environmental challenges.

6. Successful innovations and adaptations in nature become integrated into behaviours, traits, and genetic makeup of the species through the process of evolution.

7. Ecosystems in nature then continue to maintain a certain level of stability over time, characterised by a balance of species interactions, resource availability, and environmental conditions.

This has been a cyclic process through the billions of years. Each cycle from 1 to 7 must have lasted millions of years. Now, let us come back to our timescale and look at another example, that of an eagle, an annual transformation cycle from nature.

1. Initially, the eagle may validate the old status quo by relying on its existing feathers for flight. It's comfortable with its current state and sees no immediate need for change.

2. As the eagle encounters challenges or limitations with its current feathers, such as wear and tear, inability to fly at optimal levels, or facing new environmental pressures, it probably experiences a shakeup.

3. Initially, the eagle may resist the idea of shedding its old feathers. It might fear the discomfort of shedding its familiar feathers or worry about its ability to fly with new feathers. Survival possibly makes the eagle overcome this resistance.

4. As the eagle begins the shedding process, it enters a phase of confusion and chaos. It must navigate through the discomfort of losing its old feathers and adjusting to the feeling of being without them. This transition period requires resilience and adaptability as the eagle learns to cope with the changes in its appearance and flight dynamics.

5. During shedding, the eagle may explore new solutions to maintain its ability to fly. It might seek out alternative sources of support, such as temporary shelters or assistance from other eagles. Generating transformation ideas involves thinking creatively and resourcefully to adapt to the challenges presented by shedding.

6. Finally, the eagle integrates and practices its learning by adapting to its new feathers. It undergoes a period of adjustment and practice, learning to manoeuvre and soar with its transformed feathers. Through consistent effort and practice, the eagle becomes proficient in using its new feathers to retain its ability to fly.

7. Once again, the eagle may validate this status quo by relying on its existing feathers for flight. It's comfortable with its current state and sees no immediate need for change.

Just like eagles, even other birds, arthropods, reptiles, fishes, etc., from our natural world transform by shedding or adapting their body parts. Even individuals, teams, and organisations, being part of the same nature, also ADVANCE and evolve, as has been the case with life on our planet earth. The transformation, even in the case of individuals, teams, and organisations too, has phases, like the ones in our evolution and the ones in the case of an eagle. We have noticed, with our clients, that transformations take about six months to ADVANCE followed by a six-month period of just SUSTAIN before the next ADVANCE cycle, with the CORE being the foundation throughout.

Access Old Status Quo: A comprehensive assessment for establishing a common understanding of the reality is mandatory before embarking on any transformation journey and is an important leadership competency. We can compare this step with the navigation system first establishing the current position.

Detailed Goal Setting: It is obvious that setting SMART (Specific, Measurable, Achievable, Relevant, and Time-Bound) goals is quite normal these days. However, the comprehensiveness of the goals, another important leadership competency, especially when embarking on a transformation journey, is essential for favourable transformation outcomes.

Vanquish Resistance: Continuously reinforcing reality along with benefits is the key to vanquishing resistance, which is the most important leadership competency. We can say that about 1/3 of who we are is coded in our genes and comes from our ancestors. The remaining 2/3 of who we are is defined through our experiences as we grow up. Each experience adds to the wisdom of our subconscious mind to make us survive, making us reproduce and care for our progeny, making us a part of a group(s) for our own protection, and lastly, make us part of the evolution of life. These experiences create filters as we perceive, think, decide, and act. We can call these filters collectively the mindset. Our subconscious, accustomed to inertia, perceives the change we consciously seek as a threat. Consequently, it generates various intricate justifications in our minds to resist embracing the change. Such resistance is a common experience for anyone. The only way of changing the mindset for vanquishing the resistance is by creating new experiences in a safe environment. We have tried various methodologies to achieve this, and over the various assignments that we have done, gamifying the discussion with a contextual hint for an individual task combined with a contextual collective task for reinforcing the insights generated, has been most effective with a whopping 20x productivity for changing the mindset and culture for vanquishing the resistance.

Address Confusion: It is normal for people to get confused when the resistance to change is vanquished. This state of mind is again very normal since our subconscious wouldn't have sufficient memories from the new context to make us succeed, the main objective of our subconscious. Therefore, close handholding with detailed instructions, even with micromanagement, is the only solution for addressing confusion. Strategy Detailing with KPI (Key Performance Indicator) Hierarchy, Clockspeed and Owner, Establishment of -1/0/+1/+2/+3 Rolling Plans by the KPI Owners and Team Role Description and Competency Mapping or SET (**S**trategy Detailing – **E**stablishing Rolling Plans – **T**eam Role Description) for short has been our approach to addressing the confusion, an important management competency.

Nurture Learning: Unlike formal education, in companies the environment and context are extremely important to nurture learning. However, in most cases, the learning is delivered too soon in the transformation journey, with the assumption that the learning will catalyse the transformation. In our experience, imparting learning at this early stage creates even more resistance, leading to frustration and, in fact, tending to discredit the learning. Only when the CORE is strong and SUSTAIN is in place, with everyone being clear of their contribution, does the learning make sense. This is the time when everyone is anxious to learn. Since unlearning is integral to learning with adults, the Socratic method of discussions and debates is the most effective training strategy to **U**pgrade know how and do how with **P**rocess Description and Fullkit Template – UP for short.

Consolidate Learning: This is the most important phase for sustaining new learning and the wonderful improvements done. A strong CORE and SUSTAIN are the prerequisites for consolidating the learning, especially using the homework defined during the Socratic learning sessions. RUN (**R**outine Performance Reporting – **U**p-to-date Drill Down Predictive Scoreboards – **N**avigating towards the plan by deciding actions) is our approach to consolidate the learning, the most important management competency, while realising the intended transformation outcomes. People naturally improve their confidence to confront more challenges when they succeed with the learning, is our belief.

Establish New Status Quo: The last phase after strengthening the CORE to SET UP and RUN is to stabilise the new status quo for about six months SUSTAIN, before another comprehensive assessment of the new current reality, to ADVANCE again. ADVANCE naturally develops leadership and management competencies for stabilising and creating a new baseline to ADVANCE and further evolve.

In this chapter, the good practices of exceptional leaders and world-class companies, ADVANCE and SUSTAIN with CORE, are explained in a different manner, but in essence, it is just old wine in a new bottle. However, the thorough implementation and consistent practice of CORE, SUSTAIN, and ADVANCE have been our discovery which is explained in the next chapters. Continue reading the next chapters to learn, appreciate and implement the wisdom we have gained for pursuing prosperity. This wisdom is the essence of doHow®, a Socratic Learning Methodology created by me for implementing ADVANCE and SUSTAIN with CORE and enabling individuals, startups, and companies to prosper.

Homework:

With whom do you want to share your insights on CORE, SUSTAIN, and ADVANCE?

Who will be your accountability buddy for handholding and implementing your insights?

How are you practising CORE, how robust is your SUSTAIN, and when and how do you ADVANCE?

Sales and Operations

Sales and operations are fundamental components of a company's success, intertwining cash flow management, providing work for the entire organisation, meeting market needs, and fulfilling the company's mission. Cash flow is the lifeblood of a business, ensuring that it has the necessary funds to operate, invest, and grow. Sales drive this cash flow by generating revenue through the fulfilment of customer needs. Operations, on the other hand, ensure that the goods and services provided meet quality standards and are delivered efficiently, creating value for customers. Together, sales and operations create a seamless workflow that supports the entire organisation, aligns with market demands, and fulfils the overarching mission of the company.

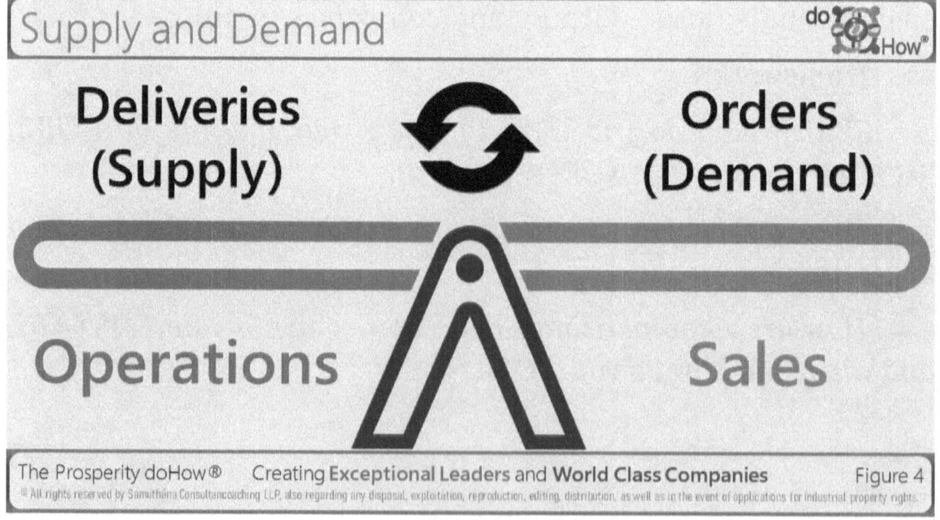

The Prosperity doHow® Creating Exceptional Leaders and World Class Companies Figure 4

The CORE, SUSTAIN, and ADVANCE are the basic enablers for both sales and operations.

Introducing Saanvi, a budding management trainee in her early 20s who thrives on the excitement of meeting new people and prospecting. Saanvi's energy and passion for building relationships help drive the company's revenue and ensure a steady stream of business. On the other side, we have Tanaka, a seasoned CEO with hands-on expertise in sales and operations, who finds joy in continual improvements and operational excellence. Tanaka's focus on refining processes and ensuring efficiency complements Saanvi's efforts, ensuring that the promises made during sales are consistently delivered with high quality. Together, Saanvi and Tanaka engage in a vibrant discussion on the synergy between sales and operations, exploring how their roles intersect to drive the company's success. Both engage in a discussion on a very important similarity in sales and operations.

Saanvi: Tanaka, why do you call sales and operations the "Siamese Twins of Business"?

Tanaka: Great question, Saanvi! Sales and operations are like Siamese twins because they're inseparable and share a common outcome: delivering quality. Sales brings in the orders, and operations fulfil them with products or services. Both are essential for the lifeblood of any business—cash flow. Think of them as two sides of the same coin; without one, the other can't thrive.

Saanvi: What about the role of hope in managing these extremely critical areas?

Tanaka: Hope can be the biggest enemy here. Imagine knowing by midday that today's goals won't be met. Often, managers rely on hope that things will turn around, much like waiting for a miracle in the second half of a sports game. But hope alone isn't a strategy. It's crucial to take a break for introspection and address the issues head-on for diagnosing and resolving the challenges in the specific tasks rather than just hoping for the best.

Saanvi: Can you elaborate on the specific tasks involved in sales and operations?

Tanaka: Sure! Sales is like a bustling marketplace where you need to prospect, make calls, send emails, build funnels, seek quotations, prepare offers, submit proposals, follow up, negotiate, and close deals. It's also about updating customer profiles, creating reports, and attending meetings. Each task is a step in the dance of winning and retaining customers.

On the other hand, operations are like the backstage crew of a theatre production. They handle new product introductions, production planning, sourcing, supply chain management, process engineering, production control, maintenance, quality assurance, logistics, updating ERP data, and creating reports. Just like in a play, every role is crucial for a flawless performance.

Saanvi: Both areas seem critical. How do they impact the business?

Tanaka: Absolutely. Both sales and operations require exceptional people skills and are directly responsible for cash flow. Think of them as the oxygen for the business. If either falter, the whole system suffers. It's like having a strong heart but weak lungs; the body can't function properly without both working in harmony.

Saanvi: What about the inherent monotony in sales and operations, now that you spoke of lungs?

Tanaka: The monotony in sales and operations is a universal challenge. For sales, the repetitive nature of prospecting, making calls, sending emails, and following up can feel like running on a hamster wheel. Every day involves similar activities, which can become mundane and lead to burnout.

In operations, the monotony comes from the routine tasks of production planning, quality assurance, maintenance, and logistics. These tasks require precision and consistency, much like a factory assembly line, where every movement is repeated day in and day out. The constant pressure to maintain high standards and meet deadlines adds to the repetitive nature, making it hard to stay motivated.

Saanvi: How do you keep these areas exciting and avoid the monotony?

Tanaka: It's much like how we need to take breaks for introspection despite our busy schedules. Regularly injecting excitement and liveliness into sales and operations can break the monotony. For example, setting simple daily goals, realistic planning with buffers, and holding daily performance reviews can become tedious. To keep things fresh, we need to add elements that boost energy and engagement, similar to how a vacation can rejuvenate us.

Saanvi: Can you share an example of how introspection helped your clients?

Tanaka: Certainly! Two of our group companies saw remarkable improvements by taking a break to introspect. One client went from achieving 85% of sales targets to consistently hitting 100% within three months. Another improved their On-Time-In-Full (OTIF) deliveries from a fluctuating 60% to a stable 100% in the same period. It's like pausing a game to reassess strategies and then coming back stronger.

Saanvi: What steps did you take to achieve these results?

Tanaka: We started by injecting excitement and getting everyone to think freely. Establishing a buy-in and a common understanding of reality was crucial. We solved some irritants hands-on, making managers' lives easier by using report data effectively. In some cases, we implemented mobile reporting. Imagine a sales officer proactively providing the latest estimates without any follow-up—this touched the hearts of area sales managers. Our fortnightly sessions combined performance reviews with team activities, keeping the energy high.

Saanvi: How did you ensure engagement and ownership?

Tanaka: We only accepted actions identified by participants within their own circle of influence, derived from their insights when pushed out of their comfort zones. It's like a team sport where each player understands their role and contributes to the collective goal. This approach ensured engagement and ownership, making the whole process more dynamic and successful.

Saanvi: That's inspiring, Tanaka. It seems like overcoming monotony in sales and operations is key to sustaining high energy and success.

Tanaka: Exactly, Saanvi. Just like taking a break for introspection in our busy lives, regular introspection and injecting excitement into the Siamese Twins of Business—sales and operations—can drive continuous improvement and keep the energy levels high.

Homework:

With whom do you want to share your insights on Sales and Operations?

Who will be your accountability buddy for handholding and implementing your insights?

How are you balancing your demand and supply equation while driving both consistently?

Leading Versus Managing

Leading and managing are two distinct yet complementary approaches essential for the success of any business. Leadership is about inspiration and vision; it involves motivating and empowering employees to achieve their fullest potential and align with the company's long-term goals. Leaders foster teamwork by creating a collaborative environment where innovation thrives and individuals feel valued and motivated. On the other hand, management focuses on effectiveness and efficiency; it is about planning, organising, and coordinating resources to achieve specific objectives. Managers ensure that day-to-day operations run smoothly, setting clear goals, monitoring progress, and solving problems as they arise. While leaders set the direction and inspire, managers create the roadmap and ensure the journey is efficient.

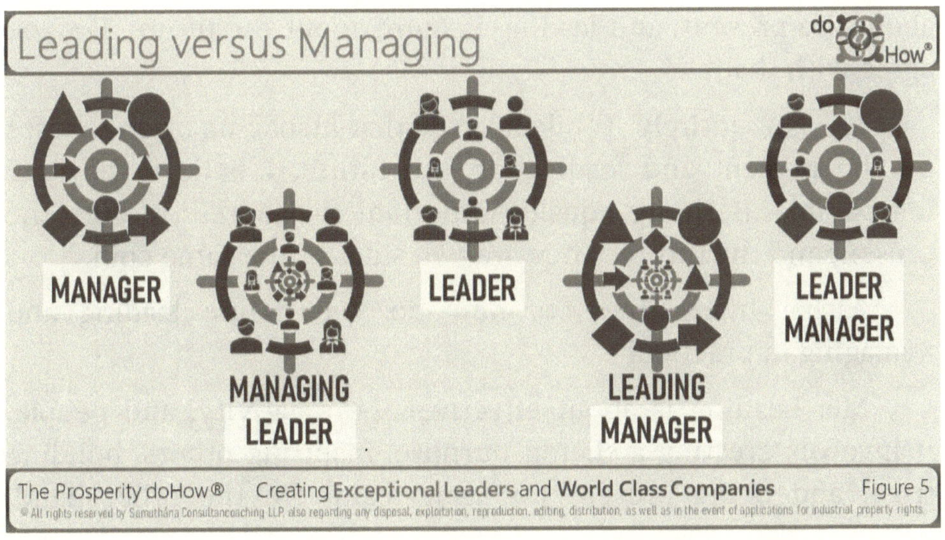

Balancing both leadership and management is crucial for building a resilient and dynamic organisation capable of adapting to change and achieving sustained success.

Both leading and managing are essential for success with the CORE, SUSTAIN, and ADVANCE.

Introducing Aisha, a fresh Human Resources graduate in her early 20s, who aspires to build a career in leadership development. Aisha is eager to understand the nuances between leading and managing and how both can be effectively applied in a business setting.

Aisha: Hi, I'd love to hear your thoughts on the differences between leading and managing. As someone aspiring to a career in leadership development, understanding these concepts deeply is crucial for me.

Me: Great question, Aisha. To put it simply, both leading and managing aim to achieve two primary objectives: thriving in the present and shaping the future. This means creating value for all stakeholders, including family, friends, the community, the government, creditors, shareholders, colleagues, customers, suppliers, and partners.

Aisha: That makes sense. Some people say managing is more about the present, and leading is more about the future. Do you agree with that?

Me: Not entirely. While it's true that managing often focuses on the present and leading on the future, I believe they are inseparable. Both are equally important for success in both the present and the future. They are two sides of the same coin.

Aisha: Interesting. So, how do you define leading and managing in practice?

Me: Leading is about effectiveness, creativity, and people. It involves creating a shared purpose, inspiring others, building trust, and being present for your team. On the other hand, managing is about efficiency, discipline, and systems. It includes setting SMART goals, detailed planning, process management, meticulous execution, regular reporting, and monitoring.

Aisha: Can someone be good at both leading and managing?

Me: Absolutely. Successful entrepreneurs and CEOs often excel in both. Great managers are essential at all levels, from the shop floor to the top floor. My belief comes from nearly forty years of experience across various countries like India, Brazil, Germany, France, Austria, Italy, Czechia, Turkey, the USA, and Japan.

Aisha: That's a lot of experience! Do you think leadership comes naturally to people?

Me: Yes, leadership taps into our human ability to dream, imagine, and strategise. However, management is a skill that requires continuous practice. It's challenging to be consistently disciplined and to choose the best path for execution excellence.

Aisha: Do you see differences in management effectiveness between developed and developing societies?

Me: Definitely. Management tends to be stronger in developed societies and weaker in developing ones. Struggling companies often face execution challenges like unclear roles, targets, and inadequate reporting. Meanwhile, comfortable multinational companies usually have these systems in place but need creative solutions to their challenges.

Aisha: I've heard about the German words fördern and fordern. How do they relate to leading and managing?

Me: They describe it perfectly. Fördern means to encourage, which is key in leadership, while fordern means to demand, which is essential in management. A good leader encourages, and a good manager demands accountability.

Aisha: How does delegation fit into this?

Me: Delegation and accountability go hand in hand and can be broken down into levels.

- Delegation Level 1: Task-based, with clear instructions.
- Accountability Level 1: Complete tasks proactively, seeking help if needed.
- Delegation Level 2: Explain the context and benefits, seeking commitment.
- Accountability Level 2: Overcome challenges to complete tasks proactively.
- Delegation Level 3: Involve team members in decision-making.
- Accountability Level 3: Recommend and seek approval for improvements before completing tasks.
- Delegation Level 4: Empower team members to make decisions within boundaries.
- Accountability Level 4: Understand the scope and boundaries to complete tasks.
- Delegation Level 5: Entrust entire projects or areas of responsibility.
- Accountability Level 5: Achieve outcomes to the satisfaction of all stakeholders.

Aisha: So, how does this apply to different types of leaders and managers?

Me: People can be just leaders, just managers, leading managers, managing leaders, or both. For instance:

- Leaders: Encourage but may not ensure accountability.
- Managers: Demand accountability but may not inspire.
- Leading Managers: Delegate at a higher level and follow up on challenges.

– Managing Leaders: Hold others accountable for outcomes but delegate specific tasks.

– Leader-Managers: Delegate and demand at the same level, creating synergy.

Aisha: How did you apply these principles in your career?

Me: I relied on both leadership and management, especially during transformations. Whether thriving in the present or shaping the future, balancing these competencies was crucial for overcoming inertia and driving change.

Aisha: This has been incredibly insightful. Thank you for sharing your wisdom!

Me: Anytime, Aisha. It's always a pleasure to discuss these important concepts. Keep thinking about where you fit and how you can balance leading and managing in your career.

Homework:

With whom do you want to share your insights on Leading versus Managing?

Who will be your accountability buddy for handholding and implementing your insights?

How are you leading and managing by balancing both for effectiveness and efficiency?

Mastering Time Management

Time management is a critical skill for any person, as it involves creating bandwidth for important activities, reducing stress, and ensuring quality time is spent on tasks that matter the most. Effective time management enables individuals and organisations to prioritise their work, focus on high-impact tasks, and meet deadlines consistently. By organising and planning how to divide time between specific activities, it becomes easier to accomplish more in less time, reduce procrastination, and avoid feeling overwhelmed. This leads to increased productivity, better work-life balance, and overall improved efficiency. Time management is not just about getting things done but doing them in a way that maximises the value and quality of the output.

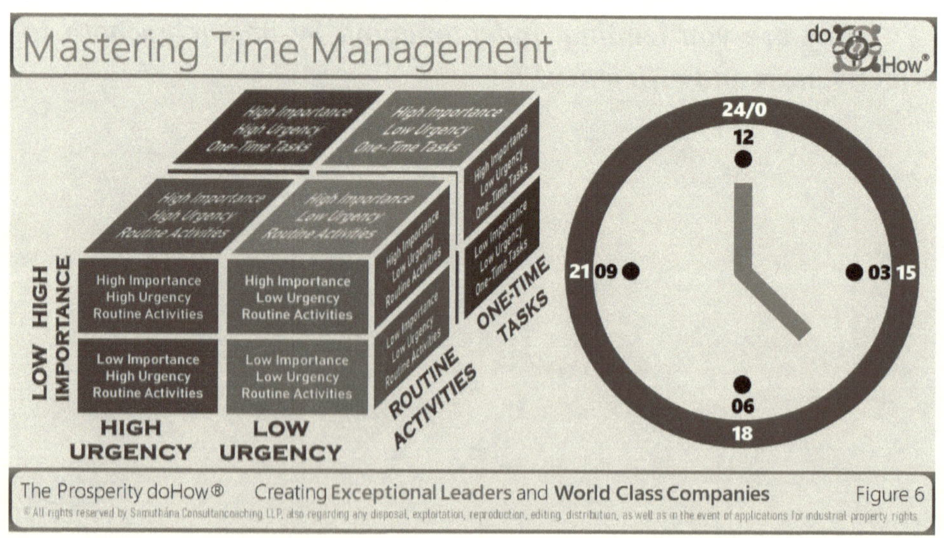

Mastering time management is necessary for basic hygiene before venturing into implementing the CORE, SUSTAIN, and ADVANCE.

Introducing Fatima, an entrepreneur in her mid-30s, who is juggling between managing her home, upbringing her kids, and running a startup. Fatima is eager to discuss how effective time management can help her balance these responsibilities and succeed in her various roles.

Fatima: I've been feeling overwhelmed with time management lately with a lot of juggling. Can you share some insights on how to handle it better?

Me: Absolutely, Fatima. Let's start with a concept from Steven Covey's book, The Seven Habits of Highly Effective People. He introduces the Circle of Influence and the Circle of Concern. It's like Krishna guiding Arjuna in the Bhagavad Gita, where you focus on what you can control and let go of what you can't. The key to effective time management is to focus on activities where you have full control and avoid worrying about things you can't influence.

Fatima: That makes sense. But how do you apply this in everyday life?

Me: Think of your day as a pie, and you have only twenty-four hours to slice it. After eight hours of sleep, you're left with sixteen hours. This time gets further reduced by personal hygiene, meals, commuting, and other commitments. You might end up with eight to twelve hours for your personal or professional goals. So, the question is, how do you make the most of this limited time?

Fatima: Yes, how do you manage that?

Me: Imagine a map with quadrants based on urgency and importance. I added a twist by also distinguishing between routine activities and one-time tasks, creating eight quadrants.

Fatima: How do you apply this quadrant model in practice? Can you explain each quadrant with some examples?

Me: Sure, let's break it down:

Me: Imagine routine activities that are both high in importance and urgency, like a garden that needs immediate watering. If you don't tend to it quickly, the plants might wither. By automating these tasks, you ensure they get done efficiently, much like setting up a sprinkler system that waters the garden at the right time.

Fatima: And what about one-time tasks that are high in both importance and urgency?

Me: Think of these as a fire that needs to be put out immediately. Having early detection systems in place, like smoke alarms, helps you address these tasks quickly before they escalate. It's about being prepared for unexpected but crucial tasks.

Fatima: What about routine activities that are high in importance but low in urgency?

Me: These are like a tree growing steadily. It doesn't require immediate attention, but you need to water and nurture it consistently. By making small, consistent efforts, you bridge the gap between where you are and where you want to be, reducing future stress. It's a long-term investment in your growth.

Fatima: And one-time tasks that are high in importance but low in urgency?

Me: Think of these as planning a big project. You don't need to tackle it all at once, but reviewing and delegating parts of it ensures it gets done effectively without becoming an emergency. It's like breaking down a large task into manageable steps.

Fatima: What about routine activities with low importance but high urgency?

Me: These are like unexpected interruptions, such as a phone call or a surprise visitor. While they need immediate attention, they aren't necessarily important in the grand scheme. Minimising their duration helps keep your productivity intact, much like quickly dealing with a minor distraction.

Fatima: And one-time tasks with low importance and high urgency?

Me: Picture this as a sudden storm. It's disruptive but not critical. By understanding why these tasks arise, you can anticipate and manage them better in the future. It's about being prepared and proactive, like having an emergency kit ready.

Fatima: What about routine activities with low importance and low urgency?

Me: These are like weeds in your garden. They don't require immediate attention, and they aren't crucial. Delegating or declining these tasks helps free up your time for more meaningful activities, much like pulling out weeds to allow your flowers to thrive.

Fatima: And finally, one-time tasks with low importance and low urgency?

Me: These are like leaves that fall in the autumn. They don't need immediate attention and can be ignored without much consequence. Deciding not to engage with them can save you valuable time, much like letting nature take its course.

Fatima: That makes a lot of sense. It's all about prioritising and managing time effectively based on the nature of the tasks.

Me: Exactly. By understanding and applying these strategies, you can optimise your time and focus on what truly matters, ensuring a balanced and productive life.

Fatima: That's quite detailed. How do you decide which strategies to use?

Me: During challenging times, I reflect on how I've spent my time and then apply the appropriate strategies for each quadrant. For instance, if I have routine high-importance tasks, I look for ways to automate them. For one-time high-urgency tasks, I set up early warnings. It's like being a chess player, always planning your moves in advance.

Fatima: What about low-importance tasks that still demand attention?

Me: It's about balancing. For low-importance but high-urgency tasks, I try to minimise their duration or find ways to avoid them altogether. It's like quickly swatting a fly that's buzzing around, not letting it distract you from your main goals.

Fatima: This approach sounds practical. How do you ensure you're always improving?

Me: Constantly reviewing and adjusting. Just like a captain steering a ship, I regularly, I mean weekly, check my course and make small adjustments to stay on track. This helps me remain productive without getting overwhelmed.

Fatima: Thank you! This has given me a new perspective on managing my time effectively.

Homework:

With whom do you want to share your insights on Mastering Time Management?

Who will be your accountability buddy for handholding and implementing your insights?

How stressed are you? How do you create and manage your time for yourself?

Mindset and Culture

Mindset and culture are foundational elements that shape the identity and performance of a business. A company's mindset reflects how individuals perceive, think, decide, act, and behave within the organisation. This collective mindset drives the culture, which encompasses the shared values, beliefs, and norms that influence how employees interact and work together. A positive and growth-oriented mindset encourages innovation, resilience, and continuous improvement, fostering an environment where challenges are seen as opportunities. Similarly, a strong organisational culture aligns employees towards common goals, enhances collaboration, and drives overall success. By nurturing both a constructive mindset and a cohesive culture, businesses can create a supportive and dynamic environment that not only attracts top talent but also retains and motivates them to excel.

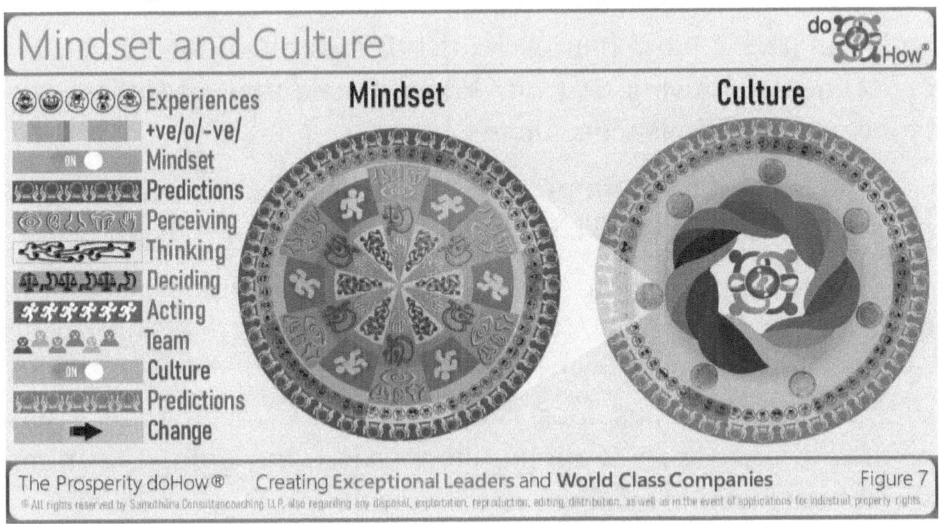

The understanding of mindset and culture is necessary to appreciate the importance of CORE in a company and to ADVANCE seamlessly.

Introducing Kabir, a digital marketing expert in his mid-30s, who works as a freelancer primarily with startup clients. Kabir is keen to delve into the impact of mindset and culture on business success, given his extensive experience in helping new ventures establish their brand and market presence.

Kabir: Hi, I'm really interested in your thoughts on the importance of mindset and culture in a business. From my experience working with startups, these elements seem crucial but often overlooked.

Me: That's a profound question, Kabir. The debate on free will has intrigued thinkers for centuries. Neuroscience, particularly the readiness potential research, offers some fascinating insights into this.

Kabir: What's the readiness potential?

Me: In the early 1960s, neurologist Hans Helmut Kornhuber discovered the "Bereitschaftspotential" or readiness potential. He found that our brain starts preparing for an action 500 milliseconds before we actually perform it, and we become conscious of this preparation only 200 milliseconds before the action happens. Later, in the 1980s, neuroscientist Benjamin Libet conducted experiments showing that our brain signals this readiness even before we consciously decide to act.

Kabir: So, our brain prepares for actions before we're aware of them? That sounds like it challenges the idea of free will.

Me: Exactly. Imagine you're about to lift your hand. According to Kornhuber's and Libet's findings, your brain is already preparing for this movement before you consciously decide to do it. This suggests our subconscious mind might be making decisions before we are aware of them, which raises intriguing questions about how much control we actually have.

Kabir: Does that mean our choices are predetermined by our subconscious?

Me: Not entirely. While the readiness potential research suggests that our subconscious mind initiates actions, it doesn't eliminate the role of conscious decision-making. Instead, it points to a complex interaction between conscious and subconscious processes.

Kabir: How do these subconscious processes work in our daily lives?

Me: Our brains are constantly gathering information, processing it, and making predictions based on past experiences. These subconscious predictions influence our behaviour and shape our choices. For example, when you catch a ball, your brain calculates its trajectory and speed without conscious effort. It's as if your subconscious mind is guiding your actions in real-time.

Kabir: So, our subconscious plays a big role in how we respond to situations?

Me: Absolutely. But this doesn't mean we lack free will. Our conscious mind still plays a role in decision-making, basically in consciously stopping the prepared response. The readiness potential research shows that our conscious awareness and subconscious predictions are deeply intertwined.

Kabir: How does this understanding of the mind affect how we change our mindset and culture?

Me: Our mindset, shaped by our memories and experiences, influences our behaviours. To change our mindset and culture, we need to consciously practice new skills and habits until they become internalised subconsciously. This gradual process transforms our behaviours over time.

Kabir: Can you give an example of how this works?

Me: Sure. Consider learning a new skill, like playing an instrument. Initially, it requires conscious effort. With consistent practice, it becomes second nature. This is similar to how we change our mindset and culture. Regular practice, especially outside our comfort zone, helps internalise new behaviours.

Kabir: How did you develop your understanding of the brain and mindset?

Me: My insights come from a blend of formal education, reading, living in diverse societies, interacting with various people, and my personal experiences. The brain, with its almost 100 billion neurons and countless connections, constantly adapts based on our experiences.

Kabir: What role do emotions play in shaping our mindset?

Me: Emotions from our experiences—whether admiration, joy, anger, or sadness—create memories that influence our mindset. These memories act as filters, shaping how we perceive, think, decide, and act. This is our reticular activating system at work, helping us navigate the world based on our unique experiences.

Kabir: How does our subconscious mind predict and influence our actions?

Me: Our subconscious mind makes real-time predictions based on sensory input and past experiences. It operates faster than our conscious mind, which becomes aware of these predictions just before execution. This allows us to react swiftly and efficiently in various situations.

Kabir: How can individuals and teams use this knowledge to improve?

Me: By regularly engaging in experiences that challenge our comfort zones, we can gradually shift our mindset and culture. For individuals, this might involve new learning experiences. For teams, collective activities like workshops and feedback sessions foster shared cultural shifts.

Kabir: Changing mindset and culture sounds like a slow process.

Me: It is. For instance, a full-day training might only result in a 0.004% change in mindset for a thirty-five-year-old. However, consistent daily practice can lead to more significant changes over time. The key is persistence and regular practice.

Kabir: But how can we effectively change our mindset?

Me: Let me illustrate with an analogy. Imagine a river flowing next to our house, causing huge problems during the rainy season with flooding. The flow of the river is like the flow of our thoughts. Now, suppose we want to change the river's course. What do you think happens if we just try to fill up the existing riverbed?

Kabir: It's a no-brainer. It will flood.

Me: Exactly. Just as the river floods, our thoughts flood and overwhelm us when we try to stop an existing behaviour abruptly. Instead, let's consider what happens if we dig a new channel to divert the river.

Kabir: The river would start flowing into the new channel too.

Me: Precisely. With the new channel, there's no more flooding near our house, and over time, the river will naturally shift its course. Similarly, when we start practising new behaviours based on new experiences, we avoid a flood of overwhelming thoughts and gradually shift to the new behaviours.

Kabir: So, the key is to create a new pathway rather than trying to block the old one?

Me: Exactly. By consistently exposing ourselves to new experiences to identify new behaviours, we carve out new channels for our thoughts to flow, leading to a gradual and natural shift in our mindset.

Kabir: How does this relate to the methodology you developed, doHow®?

Me: doHow® integrates both the analytical and emotional aspects of execution excellence. By combining these elements, doHow® helps individuals and teams achieve their vision and goals through experiential learning. Let us later discuss the inspirational persuasion gamicütion I developed for changing the mindset and culture.

Kabir: How does doHow® support this continuous improvement?

Me: doHow® facilitates new insights every two weeks and encourages daily practice through its app, promoting transparency and accountability. This helps individuals and teams steadily integrate new behaviours into their mindset and culture.

Kabir: Oh, I see. Changing mindset and culture is so easy. Isn't it?

Me: As I had explained earlier, our mind, with its purpose of protecting us, needs time to change, with new experiences to change the mindset and culture. Every new experience leads to a shock, though as elaborated in the Kübler-Ross Change Curve.

Kabir: Sounds intriguing. Can you explain how it works and the different phases?

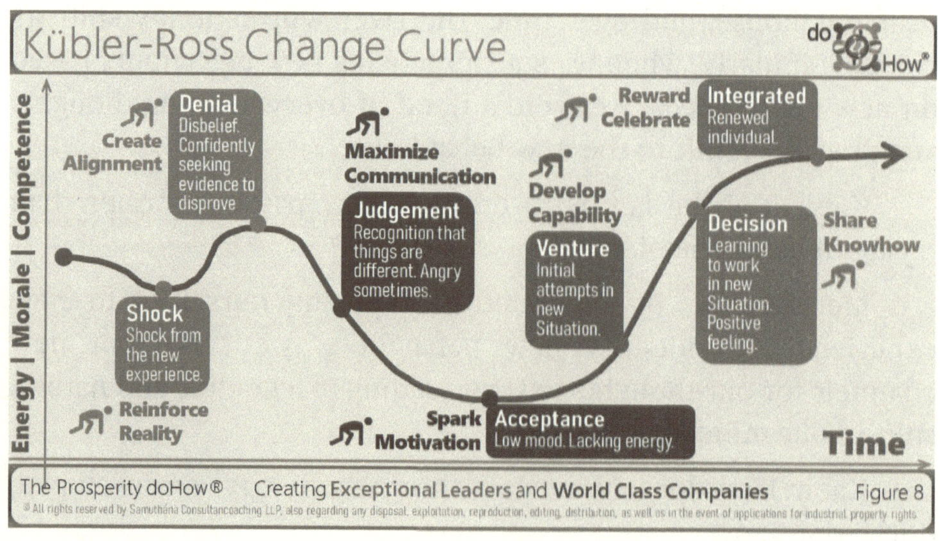

The Prosperity doHow®   Creating Exceptional Leaders and World Class Companies   Figure 8
® All rights reserved by Samuthana Consultancoaching LLP, also regarding any disposal, exploitation, reproduction, editing, distribution, as well as in the event of applications for industrial property rights

Me: Absolutely, Kabir. The Kübler-Ross Change Curve is a model that describes the emotional journey people go through when dealing with significant change. It originally came from Elisabeth Kübler-Ross's work on grief, but it applies broadly to any change. Let's go through each phase.

Kabir: What's the first phase?

Me: The first phase is Shock. Imagine you're walking through a forest and suddenly come across a clearing with an unexpected sight. The initial reaction is one of shock or surprise. This can be addressed by reinforcing the reality of the situation. It's like gently guiding someone to understand and accept what they're seeing instead of pretending it's not there.

Kabir: How does this shock phase transition to the next phase?

Me: After shock comes Denial. This is when people might refuse to accept the change, like convincing themselves the unexpected sight in the forest isn't real. They might look for evidence to disprove it. To help them move through this, you need to create alignment—showing them clearly and consistently that the change is real and unavoidable, like holding up a mirror to reflect the reality.

Kabir: What happens after denial?

Me: The next phase is Judgement, where there's a recognition that things are indeed different. This can often lead to anger or frustration, much like someone being upset when they realise their usual path through the forest is blocked. During this time, maximising communication is crucial. It's like having clear signs and guidance throughout the forest, helping them understand what's happening and why.

Kabir: What's the next phase after judgement?

Me: Following judgement is Acceptance. This is when people come to terms with the change but might feel a low mood or lack energy, like sitting down on a log, feeling weary from the walk. To overcome this, you need to spark motivation, maybe by showing them the beautiful view just ahead or the new path that leads to exciting destinations.

Kabir: What comes after acceptance?

Me: After acceptance, we enter the Venture phase. Here, people start making initial attempts in the new situation, like tentatively taking steps down the new path. Encouragement through capability building is essential here, similar to providing them with a sturdy walking stick or a map, giving them the tools and confidence to explore this new territory.

Kabir: And what follows the venture phase?

Me: Next is the Decision phase. This is when people learn to work effectively in the new situation and start feeling positive about it, like finding their stride on the new path and enjoying the journey. Sharing success stories here is powerful. It's like telling tales of others who've walked the path and reached beautiful destinations, reinforcing that they're on the right track.

Kabir: What's the final phase of this curve?

Me: The final phase is Integration. Here, the change becomes a natural part of their life, and they function as renewed individuals. It's like reaching the end of the forest and emerging stronger and more knowledgeable. This phase can be endorsed with rewards and celebrations, much like celebrating the completion of a challenging yet rewarding journey. Recognising their efforts and achievements reinforces the positive aspects of the change.

Kabir: This makes a lot of sense. It's like guiding someone through an unfamiliar forest, ensuring they understand, accept, and ultimately thrive in their new surroundings.

Me: Exactly, Kabir. By understanding and supporting people through these phases, we can help them navigate change more smoothly and come out stronger on the other side. It's all about patience, communication, and support.

Kabir: This has been really enlightening. Thanks for sharing your wisdom on mindset and culture.

Me: My pleasure, Kabir. Remember, change is a gradual process, but with persistence and the right practices, you can achieve remarkable growth in both mindset and culture.

Homework:

With whom do you want to share your insights on Mindset and Culture?

Who will be your accountability buddy for handholding and implementing your insights?

Which behaviours are you delighted with, and which do you want to change?

Stakeholder Analysis

Stakeholder analysis is a critical process that helps businesses identify, understand, and engage with the various individuals and groups that have an interest in the company. By analysing stakeholders, businesses can determine their expectations and work towards delighting them by creating value. This involves mapping out all stakeholders, assessing their influence and interest, and developing strategies to communicate and collaborate effectively. The ultimate goal is to build strong, positive relationships that support the company's objectives and foster a supportive network. Effective stakeholder analysis ensures that a company meets the needs of its stakeholders, thereby enhancing satisfaction, loyalty, and long-term success. It is particularly important for addressing potential conflicts and aligning the business strategy with stakeholder interests.

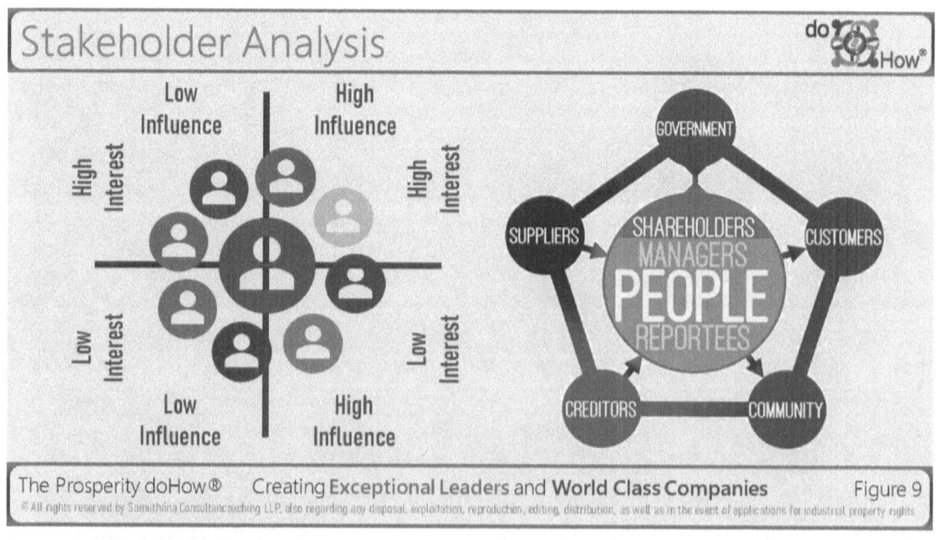

Stakeholder analysis is the foundation for effective value creation in the CORE, SUSTAIN, and ADVANCE.

Introducing Lucas, a frontline manager in his late 30s who works very hard but feels that his contributions are not appreciated. Lucas is interested in understanding how stakeholder analysis can help improve his situation and contribute more effectively to his organisation.

Lucas: Hi, I've been hearing a lot about stakeholder analysis lately. As someone who works hard but often feels underappreciated, I'd love to hear your thoughts on how this can make a difference in my role and my contributions.

Me: Sure, Lucas! Think of an organisation like a ship navigating through the ocean. Stakeholders are like the wind, waves, and currents that influence the ship's journey. To reach your destination smoothly, you need to understand these elements, their strengths, and how they impact your course.

Lucas: That's an interesting analogy. So, who exactly are these stakeholders?

Me: Stakeholders are anyone with a stake or interest in the organisation's performance. Imagine them as passengers and crew on the ship, each with their own needs and influence. This includes shareholders, managers, employees, customers, suppliers, regulators, and even the community.

Lucas: How do you figure out who these stakeholders are and what they want?

Me: It's like mapping out the sea. You identify the different groups, understand their level of influence, and consider their opinions, priorities, and concerns. You can start by naming each stakeholder and classifying them based on their role, such as a shareholder, customer, or regulator.

Lucas: Okay, and what do you do after identifying them?

Me: You need to understand their context and expectations. For example, why is a particular stakeholder involved? What are their dreams and ambitions? How do they perceive the organisation? It's like understanding each crew member's background and what they bring to the journey.

Lucas: That makes sense. But how do you prioritise their demands?

Me: It's a balancing act, like adjusting the sails to different winds. You assess their level of interest and influence. High-interest and high-influence stakeholders require more engagement, like seeking their guidance and involving them in decision-making. For those with lower interest and influence, minimal contact might suffice.

Lucas: Can you give me a more detailed example?

Me: Sure! Let's say you have a customer named Sarah. She's a high-interest, high-influence stakeholder because her feedback directly impacts product improvements and sales. You need to engage with her thoroughly, seek her guidance regularly, and keep her informed about developments. On the other hand, a low-interest, low-influence stakeholder might be a distant supplier who you only need to update occasionally.

Lucas: It sounds like a lot of work. How do you ensure everyone's expectations are managed?

Me: It is a bit like a symphony orchestra, where every instrument must be in harmony. You need a clear strategy to manage each stakeholder based on their interest and influence. Regularly sharing developments with medium-interest, high-influence stakeholders or keeping high-interest, low-influence stakeholders completely informed helps maintain balance.

Lucas: How do you get everyone in the organisation on the same page about stakeholder management?

Me: It's about creating a common understanding, like ensuring every crew member knows the navigation plan. During workshops, we collectively discuss stakeholder expectations, aiming for a win-win outcome. This alignment ensures that everyone is working towards delighting their stakeholders, not just satisfying them.

Lucas: Why is delighting stakeholders so important?

Me: Imagine two ships with equally skilled crews. The ship that delights its passengers will have a more loyal and supportive crew and passengers, leading to smoother sailing. Similarly, in a company, delighting stakeholders often sets you apart from the competition and leads to greater success.

Lucas: I see. So, understanding and managing stakeholder expectations is crucial for long-term success.

Me: Exactly, Lucas. It's the compass that guides you through turbulent waters, ensuring that you not only reach your destination but do so with the support and satisfaction of everyone involved.

Lucas: Can you explain how this would look in a company?

Me: Ah, Lucas, imagine an orchestra. Each musician represents a stakeholder. For the music to be harmonious, every musician's part must be considered. Similarly, in any organisation, whether it's a service company, manufacturing firm, or design studio, the goal is sustainable value creation for all stakeholders. It's like ensuring every musician is playing in sync.

Lucas: That makes sense. So, who are these stakeholders in a company?

Me: Let's break it down. The most straightforward stakeholders are the customers—they're the audience buying tickets to our concert. Then, we have the employees, the musicians actually performing. Shareholders are like the concert's sponsors, and partners are the fellow bands or orchestras we collaborate with. These groups are easy to identify; we usually know them by name, and then there are the regulators too.

Lucas: But there's more to it than just these groups, right?

Me: Absolutely. The plot thickens with societal stakeholders, who are like the wider community benefiting from the concert indirectly. They aren't directly involved but still expect value. Think of them as the local community enjoying the free open-air concert. Our job is to map out all these stakeholders, especially those in society, to ensure we're meeting their expectations.

Lucas: How do you determine what value to provide for such a diverse group?

Me: It's like cooking for a diverse group of friends—everyone has different tastes. Some stakeholders might want a financial return of 15%, others might be happy with 2%. Similarly, in a community, one group might appreciate a company building a school, while another values healthcare support. Understanding these varying expectations is key.

Lucas: That sounds challenging. How do you even start mapping and analysing these stakeholders?

Me: Think of it like creating a family tree. Start with the organisation itself—the immediate family—employees, management, and so on. Next, consider the extended family, like the corporate headquarters, with functions like finance and marketing. Beyond the family, we have the broader community—regulatory bodies, customers, suppliers. It's crucial to personify these stakeholders to know exactly whom to interact with.

Lucas: So, it's like knowing your neighbours in a big apartment complex?

Me: Exactly. And just like in an apartment complex, we need to keep the peace and maintain good relationships. For instance, in a city like Bengaluru, companies contribute to the community by maintaining public spaces or supporting local schools. These actions help build the city's brand and meet societal expectations.

Lucas: What about the specific needs of different stakeholders?

Me: Think of it as catering to a party. Some guests might need vegetarian options, others might want gluten-free. Regulatory bodies, for example, expect compliance with laws, while local communities might want environmental initiatives. Each group has its own needs, and we have to meet them to create sustainable value.

Lucas: And how do you know if you're meeting these expectations?

Me: Imagine running a restaurant—you'd regularly seek feedback from customers. Similarly, we conduct quarterly self-assessments to gauge stakeholder satisfaction. This helps us understand perceptions and tweak our efforts to ensure we're creating the right value.

Lucas: It sounds like a continuous effort.

Me: It is, but it's essential for the long-term success of any organisation. Just like Toyota or Tata, who aim to enhance the quality of life in their communities. It's about creating value not just for the shareholders, but for everyone involved.

Lucas: Thanks for the insightful conversation!

Homework:

With whom do you want to share your insights on Stakeholder Analysis?

Who will be your accountability buddy for handholding and implementing your insights?

How well are you managing and delighting your stakeholders?

Prosperity Chakras

Prosperity Chakras serve as a strategic framework for diagnosing the health of a business and identifying areas that need improvement. Much like the energy centres in the human body, prosperity chakras represent critical aspects of a company's operations and overall performance. By diagnosing these areas, businesses can pinpoint their weakest links and take targeted actions to strengthen them. This approach allows for a systematic assessment of current challenges and opportunities, enabling companies to prioritise their next steps effectively. Identifying and addressing these weak points is crucial for sustaining growth, enhancing efficiency, and ensuring long-term success. The concept of prosperity chakras provides a holistic view of the business, helping leaders make informed decisions and drive continuous improvement.

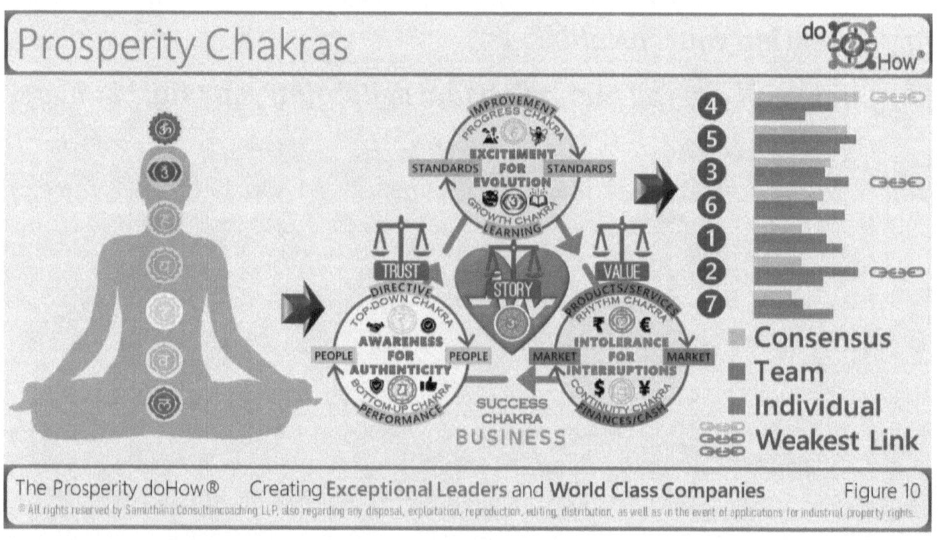

The CORE, SUSTAIN, and ADVANCE are initiated with the prosperity chakras.

Introducing Aryan, a business excellence champion in his mid-40s, who is in search of a method to quickly assess a company's strengths and weaknesses. Aryan is eager to explore the concept of prosperity chakras to enhance his ability to evaluate and improve business performance.

Aryan: Hi, I'm fascinated by the idea of prosperity chakras. As someone who often needs to quickly assess the state of a company, I'd love to hear your thoughts on how this concept can be applied effectively.

Me: Prosperity chakras are a concept I've developed to help businesses achieve holistic health and success by drawing parallels with the human chakra system. Just as our well-being depends on the balanced flow of energy in our chakras, a business's prosperity depends on the continuous flow of various elements like materials, money, information, knowledge, and emotions.

Aryan: That's fascinating! How did you come up with this idea?

Me: It all started back in the mid-1990s when I was working with Bosch in Curitiba, Brazil. We launched an initiative called CIP2000 to implement Total Quality Management (TQM). I led a cross-functional productivity team to explore ways to improve productivity across our plant. This was my first experience in setting up a baseline to initiate transformation by getting everyone on the same page.

Aryan: So, how did you transition from TQM to the idea of prosperity chakras?

Me: During a visit to our plant in Turkey in early 2000, I was given a pocketbook on the Business Excellence Model by EFQM (European Foundation for Quality Management). This model extends TQM principles to create value for all stakeholders. The EFQM model's thorough assessment process inspired me to think about a quicker and more accessible way to establish baselines and drive improvement, especially for smaller businesses.

Aryan: How did you address the challenges faced by smaller businesses?

Me: About ten years ago, the Government of India launched the ZED (Zero Effect Zero Defect) model, which is simpler and technology-enabled. I was trained as an assessor and found this model to be comprehensive yet much faster to implement. However, I still wanted to create an even quicker solution, which led me to define flows in a company as prosperity chakras based on human energy centres, or chakras.

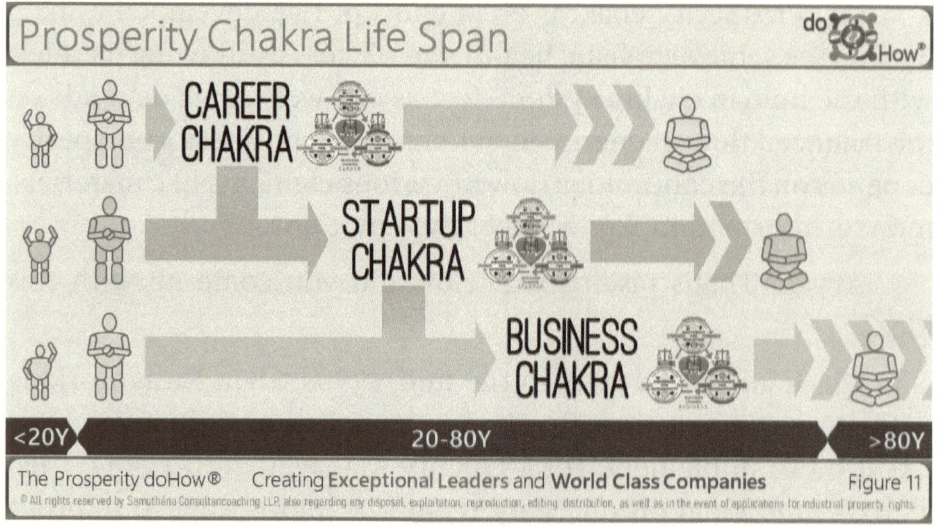

Aryan: I've been really curious about your concept of prosperity chakras. Can you explain how they work?

Me: Absolutely, Aryan. The idea of prosperity chakras is inspired by the human chakra system. Just as balanced chakras lead to personal well-being, a seamless, balanced flow in business chakras leads to a prosperous career, startup, and business. When these chakras flow harmoniously, value is created, trust is built, and inspiring stories are generated. It's all about fostering an agile or growth mindset and culture.

Prosperity	Career	Startup	Business
Ecosystem	Society	Market	Market
Robust Foundation	Contribution	Solution	Products/Services
Prosperous Livelihood	Remuneration	Investment	Finances/Cash
People	Colleague	Partner	People
Directive	Request	Order	Directive
Performance	Fulfill	Deliver	Performance
Status	Practices	Version	Standards
Convincing Change	Improvement	Development	Improvement
Perceiving Unseen	Learning	Learning	Learning

The Prosperity doHow®   Creating **Exceptional Leaders** and **World Class Companies**   Figure 12

Aryan: OK. I get it. But why have you further detailed them as career, startup, and business chakras?

Me: Good question. The prosperity chakras set the framework for creating actionable chakras. Career chakras for identifying the weakest link hindering a career, Startup chakras for finding the weakest link hindering the launch of a startup or a new product or a new version of an existing product in a company, and the Business chakras for discovering the weakest chakra impeding sustainable profitable growth.

Aryan: That sounds intriguing. Can you break down the different chakras and their roles in a business context?

Me: Sure! Let's start with the Rhythm Chakra. This chakra is all about value creation for the ecosystem and establishing a robust foundation. It ensures the seamless flow of value through stable and capable processes linked by clear, reciprocal handshakes. Closed-loop controls are crucial here to maintain a continuous flow.

Aryan: So, it's about creating a strong base. What about the next one?

Me: The Continuity Chakra represents the flow of compensation by the ecosystem derived from the value created, ensuring a prosperous livelihood. When value flows seamlessly from and to the ecosystem, it leads to sustainable prosperity. Together, the Rhythm and Continuity chakras create value.

Aryan: How do you ensure these flows are seamless?

Me: Our approach involves crafting a value stream with stable processes and practices, linked by clear handshakes. Additionally, closed-loop controls guarantee a seamless flow.

Aryan: Interesting. What about the other chakras?

Me: The Top-down Chakra reflects the flow of directives and personal power, while the Bottom-up Chakra symbolises performance driven by caring motivation. Trust is built when these flows are seamless, moving to and from the people involved.

Aryan: How do you foster this trust?

Me: We work on stakeholder expectations, reality assessment, strategy development, execution planning, regular reporting, problem-solving, and one-on-one dialogues. This comprehensive approach enables trust-building and seamless teamwork.

Aryan: That makes sense. What about improvements and learning?

Me: The Progress Chakra embodies the flow of improvements by convincing others to embrace change. The Growth Chakra signifies the flow of learning by perceiving the unseen. Together, these chakras create inspiring stories when they flow seamlessly.

Aryan: How do you drive continual improvement and learning?

Me: We focus on progressive learning through cycles that cover product or solution development, process improvement, people development, performance enhancement, productivity boosts, programming for automation, and overall progression. This approach ensures continuous improvement and learning.

Aryan: And the final chakra?

Me: The Success Chakra involves the flow of wisdom with an evolving mindset and culture that is intolerant of interruptions in value creation, aware of authenticity in trust building, and excited about evolution in generating inspiring stories. It ties all the other chakras together, ensuring a continuous flow of success.

Aryan: This is all very enlightening. How do you assess these chakras in a business?

Me: We have a quick assessment method with simple 'Yes' or 'No' questions for each chakra. The weakest chakra, identified by the most adverse answers, becomes the focus for improvement. This process, which takes about fifteen minutes, is followed by a detailed discussion to reach a common understanding and consensus, in about two hours.

Aryan: Can you give an example of this in action?

Me: Sure. For one client, the initial assessment showed that working capital was the weakest area. Through team discussions, they discovered role and goal clarity was more critical. Ultimately, the consensus highlighted deviations from standards as the focus area. Within three months, they not only met their targets but also resolved other issues, working cohesively on the identified focus area.

Aryan: That's impressive! So, balancing these chakras really helps businesses thrive?

Me: Absolutely. When the flows in these chakras are balanced and continuous, businesses can achieve holistic health and sustainable success.

With whom do you want to share your insights on Prosperity Chakras?

Who will be your accountability buddy for handholding and implementing your insights?

How have you established a common understanding of your weakest chakra?

Progressive Maturity Scale

The Progressive Maturity Scale is an invaluable tool for businesses aiming to understand their current level of development and chart a path for future growth. This scale helps organisations assess where they stand in terms of capabilities, processes, and overall maturity. By providing a clear picture of the present state, it identifies areas for improvement and sets benchmarks for progression. The scale is designed to guide businesses from basic levels of operation to advanced stages of excellence, ensuring a structured and strategic approach to growth. It emphasises continuous improvement and adaptation, enabling companies to enhance their competencies, optimise processes, and achieve higher levels of performance. Understanding and utilising the Progressive Maturity Scale allows businesses to set realistic goals, track their progress, and achieve sustainable success.

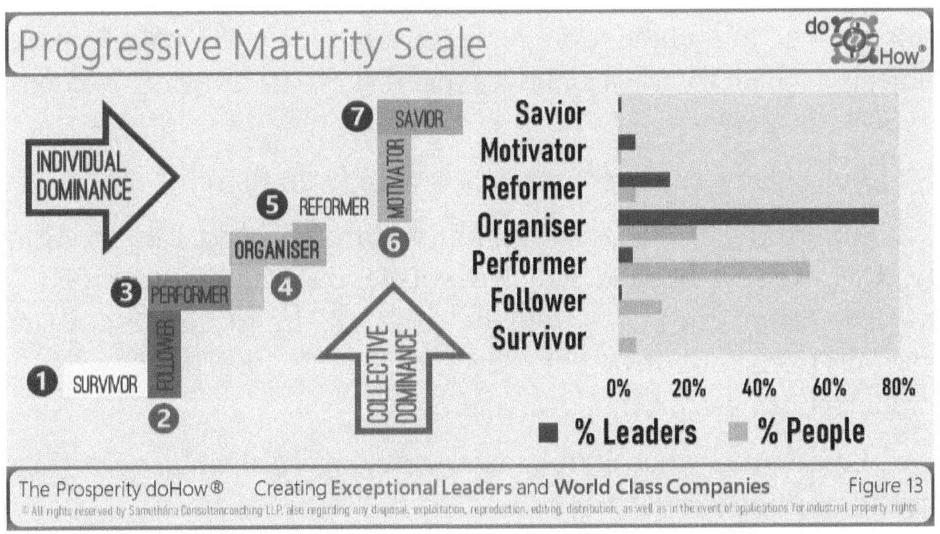

The Progressive Maturity Scale shows the maturity of the CORE, SUSTAIN, and ADVANCE in a company.

Introducing Luisa, a Learning and Development Executive in her early 30s, who specialises in competency development. Luisa is keen to discuss the Progressive Maturity Scale and its application in enhancing organisational growth and development.

Luisa: Hi, I'm really intrigued by the concept of the Progressive Maturity Scale. As someone focused on competency development, I'd love to understand how this scale can be used to guide businesses in their growth journey.

Me: Great question, Luisa! The Progressive Maturity Scale is like a map that helps organisations understand their current level of development and identify the next steps for growth. It's similar to the star ratings you see on eCommerce platforms for products or hotels, which give you an idea of quality based on customer reviews. But here, it's used to guide development and measure progress.

Luisa: That makes sense. Can you explain some of the different maturity models you've come across?

Me: Sure. My first encounter with a maturity assessment was back in 1986 during an annual appraisal. The scale ranged from 1 to 5, where 1 was "Not Fit" and 5 was "Exceptional." Over time, this evolved to include more nuanced descriptors to make it more objective, like "Always below expectation" to "Always exceeds expectation."

Luisa: How did these models evolve from there?

Me: In the 1990s, the Capability Maturity Model Integration (CMMI) was established, which has six levels, from 0 (Incomplete) to 5 (Optimising). It's widely used to build process-based organisations for consistent outcomes, laying the groundwork for modern business process management.

Luisa: And what about manufacturing companies? Do they use something similar?

Me: Yes, they often use the 5S model, which mirrors the CMMI model with levels from 0 (Disorganised) to 5 (Sustained). There are also business excellence models from the 2000s with five stages, and the ZED (Zero Effect Zero Defect) model developed by the Government of India for manufacturing uses a similar five-level scale.

Luisa: These sound pretty complex. Do they require a lot of expertise to implement?

Me: They do require some expertise for accurate assessment. That's why I created the Progressive Maturity Scale, which is simpler, intuitive, and is inspired by developmental psychology, particularly the Spiral Dynamics (SD) model. It combines elements from CMMI and SD to define seven maturity levels.

Luisa: Can you explain what the Progressive Maturity Scale is and why it's so significant?

Me: Of course, Luisa. The Progressive Maturity Scale is a framework that helps individuals and organisations understand their current level of development and figure out the next steps for growth. It's like the star ratings you see for products or hotels, but instead of just showing quality, it guides development and progress.

Luisa: That sounds really interesting. How does it actually work?

Me: The scale consists of seven levels, each representing a different stage of maturity. Let's break them down one by one.

Luisa: Perfect, let's start with the first one.

Me: The first level is the Survivor. At this stage, people or organisations act with ignorance of practice or competency. They become proactive only when their survival is at risk. They often assume they know a practice just because they've heard about it, believing that knowing is the same as doing.

Luisa: So, it's a very basic level of understanding and action?

Me: Exactly. The next level is the Follower. Here, there's an awareness of practice or competency. People start acknowledging their maturity and show a desire to learn and improve. They become proactive when their sense of companionship or belonging is at risk.

Luisa: It sounds like they are starting to recognise the importance of improvement.

Me: Right. Then comes the Performer. At this stage, individuals are learners of practice or competency. They become proactive when their reputation is at risk. They consciously learn new skills and make notes during discussions, showing a deeper engagement with their growth.

Luisa: So, they're not just aware anymore; they're actively learning and documenting their progress?

Me: Yes, and that leads us to the Organiser. Organisers are good in practice or competency. They become proactive when the clockwork of their processes is at risk. They perform consistently, compare benchmarks, and work in a structured and disciplined manner.

Luisa: It seems like they're focusing on consistency and structure now.

Me: Exactly. Then we have the Reformer. Reformers are fluid in their practice or competency. They become proactive when the future is at risk. They are constantly changing and improving, creating standards for comparing and scaling their work.

Luisa: They're always looking ahead and adapting to new challenges.

Me: Precisely. Next is the Motivator. Motivators act as coaches for practice or competency. They become proactive when prosperity is at risk. They trigger thinking and reflection for learning, with regular routine reporting and reviewing.

Luisa: So, they're not just improving themselves but also helping others grow.

Me: Yes, and finally, we have the Saviour. Saviours are masters of practice or competency. They become proactive when their legacy is at risk. They develop inclusive purposes, visions, values, and strategies. They also build a culture of continuous learning with regular auditing.

Luisa: Wow, they're focused on leaving a lasting impact and ensuring sustainability.

Me: Exactly. Each level represents a deeper and more integrated approach to growth and development, ensuring that progress is sustainable and meaningful.

Luisa: This is fascinating. It really gives a clear roadmap for both personal and organisational growth.

Me: It does. The Progressive Maturity Scale helps identify where you are and what steps you need to take to move forward, ensuring continuous improvement and lasting success.

Luisa: This model seems quite comprehensive. How does it help with self-assessment and organisational growth?

Me: It aligns key drivers of behaviour with maturity levels, providing a clear understanding of where individuals, teams, or organisations stand. It also validates lower levels before moving to the next, ensuring sustainable development. This avoids the common pitfall of spiking performance only during assessments.

Luisa: Can you give me an example of how this works in practice?

Me: Sure. Imagine a company assessing its maturity level. Initially, they might find they are at the "Follower" stage. By understanding this, they can focus on becoming "Performers," which involves consciously learning new skills and documenting discussions. This progression ensures they build a solid foundation before advancing to higher levels like "Organiser" or "Reformer".

Luisa: This is fascinating! It seems like a very structured way to ensure continuous improvement and growth.

Me: Exactly. The Progressive Maturity Scale provides a roadmap for development, helping individuals and organisations move forward in a structured, sustainable way.

Homework:

With whom do you want to share your insights on the Progressive Maturity Scale?

Who will be your accountability buddy for handholding and implementing your insights?

How good is your maturity in the various aspects of your work and life?

360° Goal Setting

360° goal setting is a holistic approach to performance management that encompasses comprehensive development by integrating feedback and insights from all directions—supervisors, peers, subordinates, and even self-assessment. This method ensures that goals are well-rounded, taking into account multiple perspectives to create a more accurate and fair evaluation of performance. By involving a wide range of feedback, 360° goal setting helps individuals identify their strengths and areas for improvement, fostering a culture of continuous growth and development. This approach not only enhances personal and professional growth but also aligns individual goals with organisational objectives, leading to stronger teamwork, increased engagement, and overall business success.

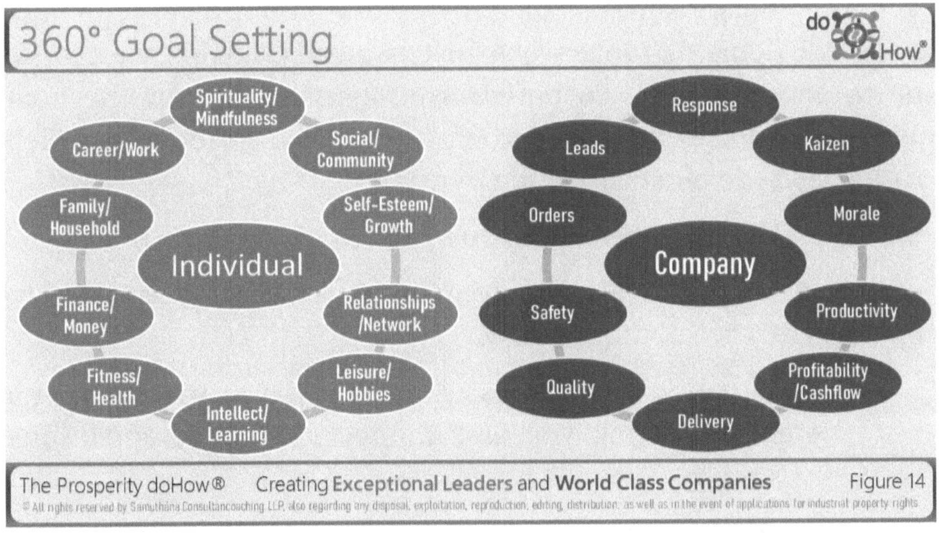

Figure 14

Goal setting makes the CORE, SUSTAIN, and ADVANCE comprehensive.

Introducing José, the owner of a small company in his late 40s, who is eager to make a difference by building a strong and cohesive team. José is interested in exploring how 360° goal setting can help him achieve this vision and enhance his company's performance.

José: Hi, I'm very interested in learning about 360° goal setting. As a small business owner, I'm looking to build a strong team and believe this approach might be beneficial. What are your thoughts on implementing it effectively?

Me: Sure, José. Imagine goal setting as a journey where you're not just looking straight ahead but all around you. For individuals, teams, and companies, it's about understanding their reality from every angle, much like a bird's-eye view. We start by getting them to speak about their current situation from their own perspectives. As they share, an expert listens and feels their sentiments, classifying them as positive, neutral, or negative.

José: Interesting! But how does this help in setting goals?

Me: Think of it like a doctor diagnosing a patient. By understanding the most impacted areas, we can focus on setting a maximum of three crucial goals for the quarter. Additionally, each individual, team, or company assesses their level of delight in specific domains. Once we've discussed all domains, we choose the three worst ones to define aspirational goals for the next quarter. It's like tending a garden – you need to identify which plants need the most care and attention.

José: What are these domains you're talking about?

Me: For individuals, the domains range from spirituality to finance. Let's break them down:

- Spirituality/Mindfulness: Imagine this as the roots of a tree, grounding you and connecting you to something greater. It's about finding meaning beyond the material world and being present in the moment.

- Social/Community: Think of this as the branches extending outwards, connecting you with others. It's about support, belonging, and shared experiences.

- Self-Esteem/Growth: This is the sunlight that nurtures the tree, helping it grow. It involves valuing yourself, recognising strengths, and continuously improving.

- Relationships/Network: These are the leaves that flourish when you have strong connections. Relationships provide support, companionship, and collaboration.

- Leisure/Hobbies: Picture these as the flowers that add colour and joy. Hobbies allow you to unwind and explore your passions.

- Intellect/Learning: This is like the water that nourishes the tree, keeping it healthy. Continuous learning expands your mind and skills.

- Fitness/Health: The trunk of the tree represents your physical and mental well-being, supporting everything else.

- Finance/Money: Think of this as the soil that provides nutrients. Managing your resources well is crucial for stability and growth.

- Family/Household: These are the protective layers that offer support and belonging. Your family is your core support system.

- Career/Work: Finally, the overall health of the tree reflects your professional life, providing purpose and fulfilment.

José: That's a beautiful analogy. How about teams and companies?

Me: For teams, the domains are more about collective dynamics. Picture a rowing team:

- Learning: The team continuously improving their rowing techniques.

- Collaboration: Rowing in sync towards a common goal.

- Communication: Ensuring everyone knows their role and the direction.

- Trust: Believing in each other's capabilities.

- Team-first mentality: Prioritising the team's success over individual glory.

- Motivation: The drive to win the race together.

- Agility: Quickly adapting to changing currents.

- Consistency: Maintaining a steady rowing pace.

- Efficiency: Maximising speed with minimum effort.

- Effectiveness: Reaching the finish line successfully.

For companies, think of them as a complex machine:

- Response: The machine's ability to adapt to new inputs.

- Kaizen: Continuous improvement of its parts.

- Morale: The energy driving the machine.

- Productivity: Output efficiency.

- Profitability/Cashflow: Financial fuel that keeps it running.

- Delivery: Timely execution of tasks.

- Quality: Maintaining high standards.

- Safety: Ensuring all parts operate without harm.

- Orders: Processing customer requests smoothly.

- Leads: Generating potential business opportunities.

José: It sounds like a comprehensive approach. How do these discussions impact individuals and teams?

Me: Imagine a two-hour discussion as a rejuvenating retreat. For individuals, it creates a new baseline, injecting positive energy and optimism for achieving their goals. For teams and companies, these discussions are like strategic planning sessions. Each function finds ways to contribute to the aspirational goals, much like different sections of an orchestra playing in harmony to create a beautiful symphony.

Homework:

With whom do you want to share your insights on 360° Goal Setting?

Who will be your accountability buddy for handholding and implementing your insights?

How comprehensive are your goals for a prosperous work and life?

Inspirational Persuasion

Inspirational persuasion is a powerful approach that leverages free thinking to generate insights and secure buy-in for implementation. It involves motivating and influencing individuals by tapping into their values, beliefs, and emotions, fostering a deep connection with the vision and goals of the organisation. This method encourages creative thinking and innovation, allowing employees to explore new ideas and perspectives. By inspiring and persuading, leaders can drive proactive behaviour, empowering their teams to take initiative and embrace change. Inspirational persuasion is essential for fostering a culture of enthusiasm and commitment, ultimately leading to the successful implementation of strategies and achieving business objectives.

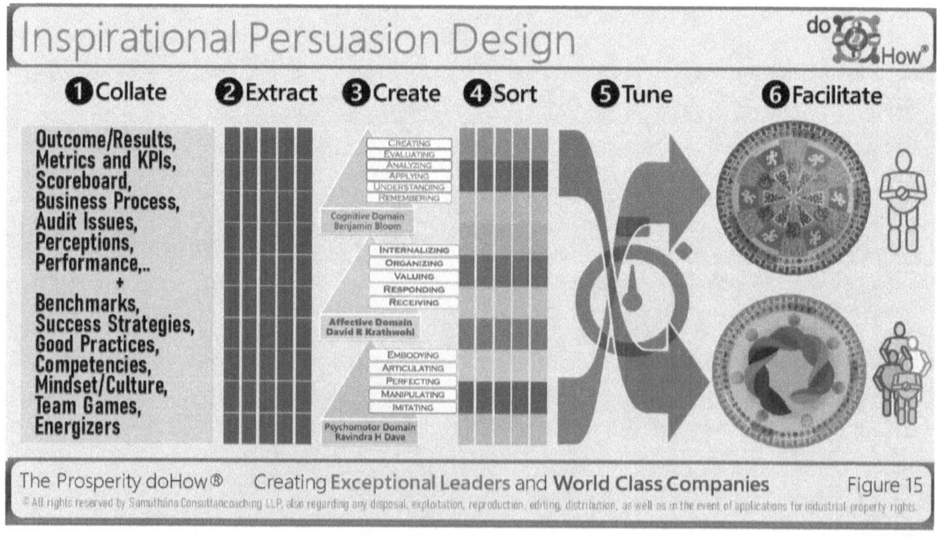

The Prosperity doHow®   Creating **Exceptional Leaders** and **World Class Companies**   Figure 15

Inspirational persuasion is the foundation for effectively implementing the CORE, SUSTAIN, and ADVANCE.

Introducing Ishaan, a change manager in his mid-50s who is seeking a solution to make people more proactive. Ishaan is eager to discuss how inspirational persuasion can be applied to encourage proactive behaviour and drive positive change within the organisation.

Ishaan: Hi, I'm really interested in understanding more about inspirational persuasion. As a change manager, I'm constantly looking for ways to make people more proactive. How do you think this approach can help?

Me: Absolutely, Ishaan! Imagine you're trying to light a campfire. You have the wood and the matches, but what you need is that perfect spark to ignite it. Our inspirational persuasion gamification is just like that spark. It's designed to get people thinking differently and to ignite the fire in their belly, helping them develop an Agile Mindset for achieving Amazing Outcomes through Execution Excellence.

Ishaan: That sounds intriguing. How exactly does this gamification work to break down departmental barriers and change mindsets?

Me: Think of it like a bridge-building exercise. We take large groups and break them into smaller teams of two, three, or four. This smaller setup unleashes the power of free thinking, just like how smaller streams converge to form a mighty river. The game revolves around handpicked contextual topics specific to the actual issues and challenges faced by a team or company. This focus helps in breaking down departmental silos and fosters discussions that lead to the desired outcomes.

For instance, we had a sales team that was struggling to meet targets. By using our gamification approach, they went from hitting only 85% of their target to consistently surpassing 100% within three months.

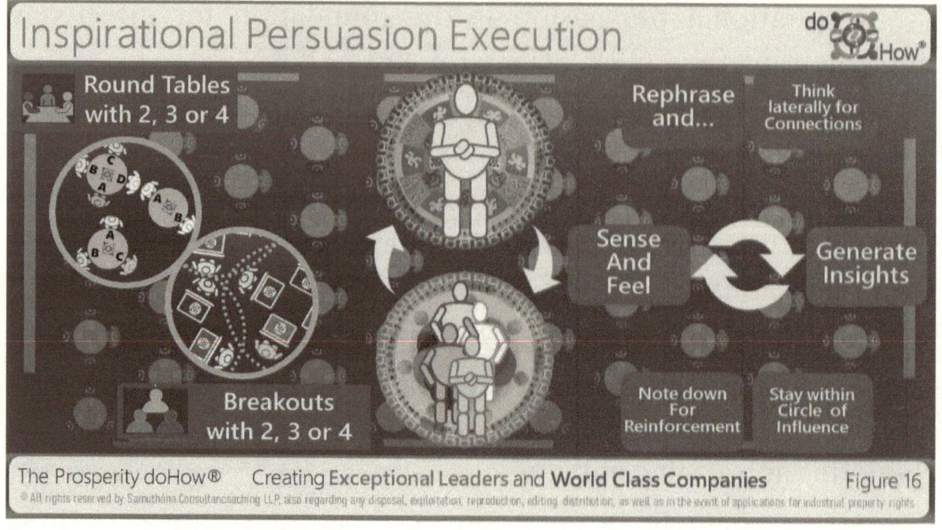

The Prosperity doHow®   Creating **Exceptional** Leaders and **World Class Companies**   Figure 16

Ishaan: Interesting! So, what kind of tasks do the participants engage in?

Me: We use a mix of individual and collective tasks, much like a symphony where each instrument plays its part before coming together for a harmonious performance. For instance, participants might be asked to position themselves on a scale from Disagree to Agree on certain topics individually. Then, in their teams, they come up with tips and tricks based on these positions.

This mix of random individual and collective tasks gets people almost continuously generating insights, which also means that dopamine is being pumped continuously, making the participants very energetic throughout the session. In another case, a company was facing issues with on-time delivery. Our approach helped them improve their on-time delivery performance from 70% to 100% in just three months.

Ishaan: That's a unique approach. How do you ensure that these discussions are meaningful and lead to an agile growth mindset?

Me: It's all about the right kind of hints and prompts. Imagine each hint as a seed planted in fertile soil. These seeds are based on thorough situation appraisals of the actual issues at hand. They trigger focused discussions and debates in a Socratic way, where participants question and build on each other's thoughts, helping them evolve an agile growth mindset.

For example, we worked with an EPC project team to achieve an all-time record performance by identifying improvement potentials and connecting the dots to understand cause-and-effect relationships.

Ishaan: And how does this impact the overall execution mindset and culture?

Me: Picture a dance where every step must be in sync with the music. Our methodology alternates between individual and collective tasks, ensuring that participants are constantly perceiving, thinking, discussing, deciding, and acting without judgement. This rhythmic pattern fosters an environment where execution excellence becomes second nature, and actions are always within the participants' circles of influence.

In another case, a company experienced a 25% year-on-year growth and a 5% increase in profitability by evolving success strategies and automating repetitive tasks.

Ishaan: How do you start the process? How do you ensure that the right issues are addressed?

Me: It all begins with understanding the context thoroughly, like a detective gathering clues. We look at outcomes, metrics, KPIs, perceptions, and more. From this gathered information, we extract key messages and formulate them as hints for various tasks. This preparation ensures that the game is always relevant and impactful. For instance, when we worked on improving leadership culture, we focused on mindset and relatedness, leading to a significant improvement in their Employee Satisfaction Index (ESI) within three months.

Ishaan: Can you give me an example of a task from the game?

Me: Sure! One task might involve participants explaining how effective it is to act proactively for any deviations and then reporting the status to their customers or superiors. Another task could be assessing and explaining how their teams perform concerning clear and open lines of communication. We also have tasks that help participants understand their role as implementers—the ones who put ideas into action—by identifying who is responsible or deputised and whether they are empowered. Lastly, participants might think of a recent problem, visualise it on a pinboard, and analyse its impact using a specific hint.

Ishaan: This sounds like a powerful tool for any organisation. What are some of the collective tasks you use?

Me: Think of these tasks as building blocks of a great structure. Participants might design a collaborative art piece, discuss and refine their daily routines, or even enact a short skit demonstrating their emotions after achieving a goal. These activities not only consolidate individual insights but also strengthen team cohesion and alignment towards common goals.

Ishaan: I can see how this would be engaging and effective. What's the final step in this process?

Me: The final step is like the grand finale of a concert. Participants conclude the session by finalising their actions based on the insights they've gathered. They note down these actions within their circle of influence, ensuring that everyone leaves with a clear, actionable plan.

Ishaan: That's brilliant! It sounds like your method really transforms the way teams approach their challenges and goals. Thanks for sharing this with me.

Me: My pleasure, Ishaan! It's all about creating that spark and watching it grow into a roaring fire of innovation and excellence.

Homework:

With whom do you want to share your insights on Inspirational Persuasion?

Who will be your accountability buddy for handholding and implementing your insights?

How are you creating an ambience of free-flowing thinking and discussing?

Key Performance Indicators

Key Performance Indicators (KPIs) are essential tools for businesses to maintain focus, declutter processes, and prioritise actions. KPIs are specific, measurable metrics that reflect critical aspects of a company's performance and success. By setting clear KPIs, organisations can concentrate their efforts on what truly matters, avoiding distractions and aligning resources with strategic objectives. KPIs help in tracking progress, identifying areas that need improvement, and ensuring that everyone in the organisation is working towards common goals. This targeted approach not only enhances efficiency but also drives better decision-making and accountability, ultimately leading to improved business outcomes.

KPI fosters focus during the implementation of the CORE, SUSTAIN, and ADVANCE.

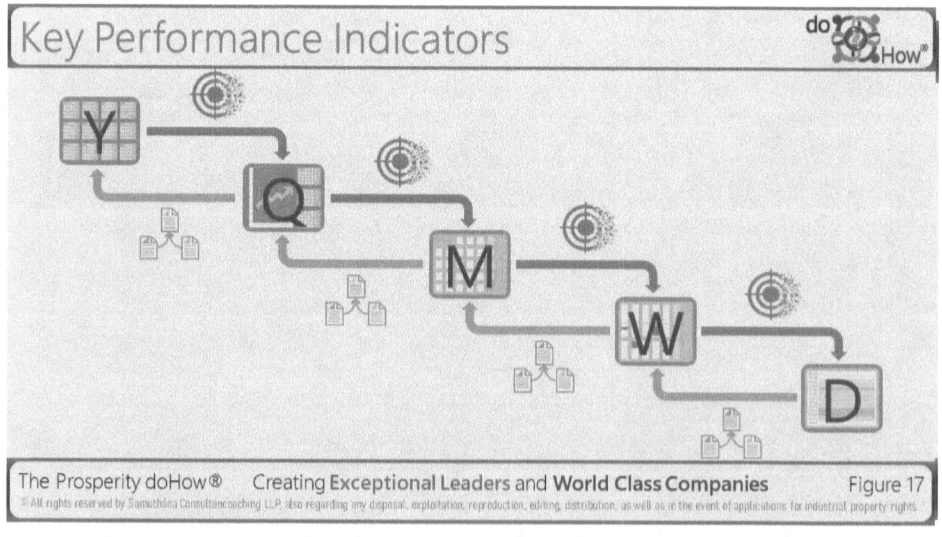

The Prosperity doHow®   Creating **Exceptional Leaders** and **World Class Companies**   Figure 17

Introducing Maria, an executive assistant to the CEO in her mid-30s, who is responsible for effectively deploying the strategies defined by the leadership team. Maria is keen to explore how KPIs can help streamline efforts and ensure the successful implementation of strategic initiatives.

Maria: Hi, I'm really interested in learning more about Key Performance Indicators. As the executive assistant to the CEO, I need to ensure that the strategies we define are effectively deployed. How can KPIs help with this?

Me: Sure, Maria! Think of KPIs as the compass that guides a ship through uncharted waters. They help organisations stay on course and reach their desired destinations. KPIs are metrics that measure performance and success, aligning with the company's strategy. It's like setting clear, measurable goals for every step of the journey.

Maria: That makes sense. But what makes a KPI truly effective?

Me: It's like preparing a recipe. The first ingredient for an effective KPI is absolute clarity on where the data comes from and how it's calculated. Imagine trying to bake a cake without knowing the exact measurements of your ingredients. For instance, if you're calculating an average, are you using daily, weekly, or monthly data? Clarity ensures consistency and accuracy.

Maria: Interesting analogy. What's next after ensuring clarity?

Me: The next step is making sure you're comparing apples to apples, not apples to oranges. Imagine a fruit market where you're comparing the prices of different types of fruit. If you compare an apple to an orange, the comparison doesn't make sense. Similarly, KPIs must be comparable across different departments or units. For example, if you're measuring sales performance, ensure that the same criteria apply across all sales teams.

Maria: I see. And how do you handle data collection for KPIs?

Me: Think of data collection like mining for gold. You need to sift through a lot of material to find the valuable nuggets. Data cleaning is crucial to analyse the outliers and ensure the integrity of your KPIs. Outliers can hide valuable insights, just like gold nuggets can be missed if you're not careful during the mining process.

Maria: That's a vivid picture. What about the timing of KPI measurements?

Me: Timing is like the heartbeat of your organisation. It's essential to measure KPIs at the right intervals—daily, weekly, monthly, or quarterly—depending on what you're tracking. For example, daily sales figures might be collected and reviewed weekly to spot trends and make timely decisions. Just like a doctor monitors a patient's heartbeat to gauge health, regular monitoring of KPIs ensures the business stays healthy.

Maria: Can you give me some examples of how KPIs are used in practice?

Me: Absolutely! Let's say you're in sales. A top-level KPI might be the total sales revenue, while a driver metric could be the number of cold calls made or follow-ups completed. It's like having a roadmap with landmarks; the driver metrics are the steps you take to reach your final destination.

For on-time delivery, a top-level KPI might be the percentage of deliveries made on time. The driver metric could be ensuring that all team members are informed, preferably twice a day, about the updated rolling plan based on the progress made. Think of it as a relay race where each runner must know when to take the baton to ensure a smooth handoff.

Maria: That really brings it to life. But I've also heard about lead and lag indicators. How do they fit into the picture?

Me: Great question! Think of lead indicators as the early warning signs and lag indicators as the outcomes. Lead indicators are like the weather forecast—they give you a sense of what's coming and allow you to make adjustments. For instance, the number of sales calls made is a lead indicator for future sales. Lag indicators, on the other hand, are like the actual weather conditions—they tell you what has happened. Total sales revenue is a lag indicator. Both are essential: lead indicators help you anticipate and act, while lag indicators show the results of those actions.

Maria: That makes a lot of sense. But how do you connect these KPIs across different levels of an organisation?

Me: This is where the KPI tree comes into play. Picture it as a family tree where each branch represents a different aspect of the organisation, all connected to a central goal. At the top, you have your main KPIs, like profitability or customer satisfaction. From there, you branch out to driver metrics, which are the specific actions and processes that influence those top-level KPIs.

For example, if your top-level KPI is profitability, a driver metric might be the percentage of budgeted expenses ordered. This driver metric could be further broken down into specific actions like timely purchase orders and efficient use of resources. It's like tracing back each leaf to its branch and then to the trunk, ensuring that every action aligns with the overall strategy.

Maria: This really ties everything together. But who ensures that these KPIs are tracked and managed effectively?

Me: That's a crucial point, Maria. Defining a KPI owner is essential. Think of the KPI owner as the captain of a ship, responsible for overseeing and monitoring the KPI to ensure it stays on course. The KPI owner ensures data accuracy, regular monitoring, and timely reporting. They are accountable for the performance and must steer actions to improve results when necessary.

Maria: And how important is the timing or clock speed for monitoring these KPIs?

Me: The clock speed is vital. It's like setting the right tempo in a musical piece. You need to decide whether to monitor and report on KPIs daily, weekly, monthly, quarterly, or yearly based on the nature of the metric. For example, sales and delivery performance might need daily tracking with weekly reviews, while strategic initiatives might be reviewed quarterly. The key is to choose a frequency that matches the flow and impact of the metric to make timely and effective decisions.

Maria: This is really comprehensive. So, what's the most important takeaway about KPIs?

Me: Just remember, KPIs are like the DNA of your organisation, capturing critical information about performance and strategy. The three key points to keep in mind are: clarity in data and calculations, ensuring comparable metrics, and setting the right measurement frequency. And don't forget the importance of using both lead and lag indicators to get a complete picture, the KPI tree to identify and connect driver metrics, and appointing a KPI owner to oversee and monitor the process. With these in place, KPIs become powerful tools for navigating towards success.

Homework:

With whom do you want to share your insights on Key Performance Indicators?

Who will be your accountability buddy for handholding and implementing your insights?

How have you cascaded the key performance indicators and clearly assigned ownership?

Rolling Planning

Rolling planning is a dynamic approach that provides businesses with the agility to respond to market fluctuations while maintaining constancy in operations. Unlike traditional static planning, rolling planning involves continuous updates and revisions to plans based on real-time data and changing circumstances. This method allows companies to stay flexible and adapt quickly to new opportunities or challenges, ensuring they remain competitive in a volatile market. At the same time, it provides a steady framework for day-to-day operations, helping to align resources and efforts with long-term strategic goals. Rolling planning ensures that businesses can navigate uncertainties with confidence, optimise their processes, and achieve sustained success.

Rolling planning makes the CORE, SUSTAIN, and ADVANCE both rigid and flexible.

Introducing Peter, a production planning manager in his late 40s, who is struggling with the pressures of bad planning and constant demands from various departments. Peter is eager to understand how rolling planning can help him manage these challenges more effectively.

Peter: Hi, I've been having a tough time with planning lately, constantly getting pulled up for bad planning. I'm really interested in learning about rolling planning. How can this approach help me improve?

Me: Great question, Peter! Imagine planning as trying to navigate through a forest without a clear path. When the terrain is stable, it's easier to map out your route. But in today's VUCA (Volatile, Uncertain, Complex, Ambiguous) world, the path is constantly changing. One of my bosses once told me, "A plan is called a plan because it can be changed." This is especially relevant now, as flexibility in planning is crucial.

Peter: So, how do you balance making commitments and fulfilling them in such a fluctuating environment?

Me: Think of a value stream as a chain of dominoes. In stable times, you can commit and plan in advance, making sure each domino falls in place perfectly. But in the VUCA world, you need to plan carefully before committing, as even one misstep can cause a chain reaction affecting downstream stakeholders. It's about finding the balance between having a stable plan and being flexible enough to adapt to changes.

Peter: That sounds challenging. What's the solution?

Me: The solution is the frozen rolling plan, Peter. Imagine it as a rolling wave where the crest is frozen while the rest keeps moving. This plan is divided into five time zones (TZ), from +3TZ to -1TZ, each representing different stages of planning and commitment. Let's start with the farthest one and move closer to the present.

Peter: Sounds good. What's the +3TZ about?

Me: In the +3TZ, we focus on the target for prioritising based on stakeholder needs with up to 40% change. It's like forecasting the weather for next month; you account for external fluctuations and prioritise what's important. This helps us anticipate major changes and align our long-term goals accordingly.

Peter: And what about the +2TZ?

Me: The +2TZ is all about forecasting for the feasibility of freezing with up to 25% change. It's like looking at the weather forecast for next week. You check the feasibility of your plans, considering higher lead times, and start preparing to lock things down as you get closer to execution.

Peter: Interesting. So, how do you handle the +1TZ?

Me: The +1TZ involves creating a frozen plan for getting the full kit ready with up to 10% change. Think of it as preparing for tomorrow's weather based on today's observations. You anticipate unknown constraints and ensure everything is ready to go, making only minor adjustments if necessary.

Peter: What happens when you get to the 0TZ?

Me: The 0TZ is where we have the frozen estimate for targeted execution with less than 5% change. This is where Murphy's Law comes into play—anything that can go wrong might go wrong. It's like having a detailed weather report for today and preparing for those last-minute surprises. This plan is solid but allows for minimal adjustments.

Peter: And finally, what about the -1TZ?

Me: The -1TZ is all about learning from the actual versus the estimate with 0% change. It's like reviewing yesterday's weather to understand what really happened. This stage is critical for understanding deviations and learning from them. It's the foundation for making better plans moving forward.

Peter: This step-by-step approach makes a lot of sense. So, how does it all come together in practice?

Me: It comes together through daily standing meetings where we review each time zone's performance and make necessary adjustments. For example, during a week in March 2022, we had specific outcomes for each day based on the frozen rolling plan.

Peter: Are there any challenges with rolling planning?

Me: Yes, of course, there are challenges as always. The biggest one is getting people to adhere to the rolling plans against all odds, especially for optimising their respective areas. With rolling planning, it is always about the team outcomes and not individual outcomes. So, there may be situations where individuals must adapt against their individual preferences. This is a clear challenge, which can be overcome by clearly and constantly explaining the simple fact that when the team wins, everyone wins.

Rolling Planning

Number of ....079 Assemblies	Learning (-1TZ)		Estimate	Plan	Forecast	Target
	Estimate	Actual	0TZ	+1TZ	+2TZ	+3TZ
16Mar2022 Wed	10	9	11	10	11	12
17Mar2022 Thu	11	10	10	10	11	12
18Mar2022 Fri	10	8	9	11	11	12
19Mar2022 Sat	9	9	11	11	11	13
21Mar2022 Mon	11	11	11	12	12	12

The Prosperity doHow®   Creating Exceptional Leaders and World Class Companies   Figure 18

Peter: Can you give me a concrete example of how this rolling planning works, say, for deliveries?

Me: Absolutely, Peter. Let's look at how we handle it during daily standing meetings over a week.

Peter: Sure, let's start with March 16th.

Me: On March 16th, we found that only nine units were delivered instead of the estimated ten. In our morning meeting, we discussed the reasons and identified absenteeism in the production line as the culprit. It's like discovering that a player missed the game, causing the team to lose points. We got everyone to sign off on the new estimates, plans, forecasts, and targets, ensuring commitment from all involved.

Peter: And what about March 17th?

Me: On March 17th, the delivery was ten units instead of the planned 11. During our meeting, we realised the delay was due to a vendor delivery issue caused by overdue payments. This is like a relay race where one runner fumbles the baton exchange. We noted why the plan and forecast were reduced by one and got everyone to sign off again, committing to the adjusted targets.

Peter: What happened on March 18th?

Me: On March 18th, only eight units were delivered instead of ten. In our meeting, we discovered a machine breakdown caused the shortfall. It's like a flat tyre during a road trip. We discussed why the estimate and forecast were reduced and ensured everyone understood the changes by signing off on the revised plans.

Peter: How about March 19th?

Me: On March 19th, we noted the forecast was reduced by one unit due to a vendor payment issue. During our meeting, it was clear that financial bottlenecks were impacting deliveries, much like a cash flow problem affecting household expenses. We got sign-offs from all stakeholders to commit to the updated plans.

Peter: And finally, what happened on March 21st?

Me: On March 21st, the plan increased by one unit while the forecast was reduced by one due to load balancing. It's like adjusting your budget after realising some expenses were lower than expected. In our meeting, we made sure everyone was aligned with these adjustments and secured their commitments through sign-offs.

Peter: So, after the week, what's the next step?

Me: After a week, we prepare a Pareto chart to analyse the undesirable effects, like the vendor payment issue. Think of it as a post-game analysis to identify the biggest challenges. We then check outstanding payments, prepare a cash flow statement, forecast payment dates, and discuss agreements with vendors. It's like recalibrating our strategy based on game-day performance, ensuring we learn and adapt for future success.

Peter: This sounds like a robust system. What's the ultimate benefit of this approach?

Me: The ultimate benefit is building a resilient organisation that consistently meets its commitments, much like a sports team that continually wins games. It instils confidence in the team and creates a culture of reliability and adaptability. By having a structured yet flexible plan, we create a system that can navigate the complexities of the VUCA world and achieve its goals.

Peter: This frozen rolling plan seems comprehensive. What's the ultimate benefit of such a detailed approach?

Me: Once you start meeting your plans and commitments consistently, it's like building a winning sports team. The organisation can embark on a journey to world-class performance, and it instils confidence in all its people. By having a structured yet flexible plan, you create a robust system that can adapt to changes and still achieve its goals.

Homework:

With whom do you want to share your insights on Rolling Planning?

Who will be your accountability buddy for handholding and implementing your insights?

How are you providing the constancy for operational excellence and the agility for market demand fluctuations?

Job Role Description

Job role descriptions are fundamental to the smooth operation and success of a business. They clearly outline the prerequisites, responsibilities, and competencies required for each position within the organisation. By defining these elements, job role descriptions ensure that employees understand what is expected of them, which skills and qualifications are necessary, and how their roles contribute to the overall goals of the company. This clarity helps in recruiting the right talent, setting performance expectations, and providing a basis for evaluating employee performance. Moreover, well-crafted job descriptions foster accountability by making it clear who is responsible for specific tasks and outcomes. They also facilitate career development by identifying the skills and competencies needed for advancement, thus contributing to a more motivated and productive workforce.

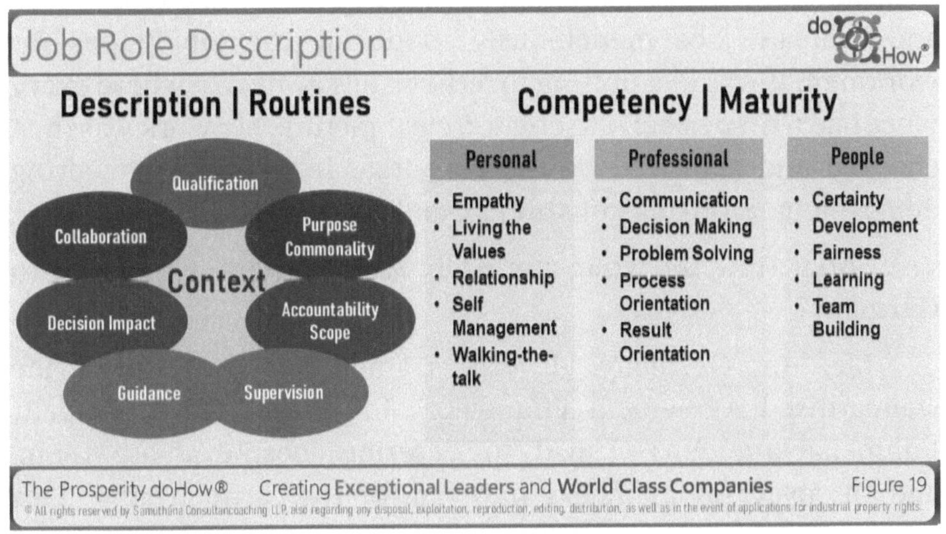

Job Role Description is the foundation for creating clockwork in the CORE, SUSTAIN, and ADVANCE.

Introducing Sofia, the CEO of a medium-sized enterprise in her late 40s, who struggles with making people accountable for their outcomes. Sofia is keen to explore how effective job role descriptions can help address this challenge and improve accountability within her organisation.

Sofia: Hi, I've been facing difficulties in making people accountable for their outcomes. I'd love to hear your thoughts on how job role descriptions can help with this issue.

Me: Absolutely, Sofia! Think of job role descriptions as the blueprint of a building. Just like a blueprint guides the construction and ensures everything is in place, a well-defined job role description guides employees and aligns their tasks with the company's goals. The first time I encountered job descriptions and evaluations was back in the 1980s during my Industrial Engineering program. It was essential for deciding job grades for workmen, ensuring everyone knew their responsibilities and roles.

Sofia: That makes sense. How did you approach job descriptions in your early days at Bosch?

Me: In Bosch, as a manufacturing engineer, I had to describe and evaluate jobs meticulously to decide the job grades for workmen. It was like putting together a jigsaw puzzle where every piece had to fit perfectly to create a clear picture. My work was then checked and approved by the corporate Industrial Engineering department, ensuring consistency and accuracy.

Sofia: How did your approach evolve when you moved to Germany?

Me: In Germany, I was trained in the nationwide standardised Agreement Framework for Wages (ERA: Entgelt-Rahmenabkommen). I had to describe jobs, evaluate them, and fit my team members into one of the tariff groups. This was like building a complex machine where each component had to be precisely placed to ensure smooth operation. Later, back in India, I got trained in the Mercer International Position Evaluation methodology to describe and fit mainly mid and senior management roles, ensuring that the right people were in the right positions.

Sofia: That sounds quite comprehensive. How do modern frameworks like the Qualification Pack – National Occupational Standards (QP-NOS) fit into this?

Me: The QP-NOS from the National Skill Development Corporation (NSDC) is an excellent tool, much like ERA in Germany. It's like having a detailed map for every industry sector, providing a solid foundation for bridging the skill gap. However, companies still need to make significant efforts to reskill and upskill their employees based on these standards.

Sofia: With so many assessment tools available, how do you determine the right fit for a job?

Me: I've encountered numerous assessments over the years, like Theory X-Y, Insights Discovery, Enneagram, MBTI, and many more. These tools are like different lenses through which you can view an individual's potential. However, they are not foolproof. An experienced leader can often provide a more accurate assessment of an individual after a short discussion or interview, much like a seasoned jeweller can appraise a gem by just looking at it.

Sofia: There seems to be a debate about the necessity of precise job descriptions versus trust and team outcomes. What's your take on that?

Me: It's a bit like driving a car. When you first learn to drive, you need clear instructions and guidance. Similarly, job descriptions provide a foundation for performance excellence. Over time, as teams become more skilled and self-managed, they can navigate without needing detailed descriptions for every task. But even self-managed teams benefit from having a clear understanding of their roles based on an initial job description.

Sofia: So, what makes an effective job role description?

Me: An effective job role description covers several key aspects that define the context of the role. Collaboration, Purpose, Accountability, Supervision, Guidance, Decision, and Qualification together define the context. Let's break them down in detail.

Sofia: Sure, let's start with collaboration.

Me: Think of collaboration as the glue that holds a team together. In a job role description, you need to outline the expected collaboration impact of the role. For example, how often and effectively should the person in this role work with others? You also look at the actual collaboration impact they've demonstrated over at least the past two years. It's like evaluating how well different parts of a machine work together to achieve a common goal.

Sofia: That's interesting. What about the purpose of the role?

Me: The purpose is the heart of the role. It defines why the role exists and how it aligns with the company's mission. You need to describe the expected individual, functional and company purpose congruence, meaning how well the role's objectives match the company's goals. Then, assess the actual purpose congruence the role occupant has demonstrated over the past two years. It's like ensuring that every piece of a puzzle fits perfectly to complete the bigger picture.

Sofia: How do you address accountability in a job role description?

Me: Accountability is about ownership and responsibility. You outline the expected level of accountability for the role, such as what tasks and outcomes the person is responsible for. You also measure the actual level of accountability shown by the role occupant over the past two years. Think of it as a scale where you balance expected responsibilities with actual performance, ensuring the person reliably meets their commitments.

Sofia: And what about supervision?

Me: Supervision is the guidance and oversight needed for the role. You describe the expected intensity of supervision, such as how often and how closely the person should be supervised. Then, compare it to the actual intensity of supervision they've received over the past two years. It's like setting the amount of light needed to nurture a plant—too much or too little can impact growth.

Sofia: What's the role of guidance in this context?

Me: Guidance is about providing direction and support. You specify the expected frequency of guidance, like how often the person should receive advice and feedback. You also assess the actual frequency of guidance they've experienced over the past two years. It's like being a mentor, ensuring that the person has the support they need to navigate their responsibilities effectively.

Sofia: How important are decision-making capabilities in a role?

Me: Decision-making is crucial. You outline the expected impact of the decisions the person in this role should make. This includes the scope and significance of their decisions. Then, evaluate the actual impact of their decisions over the past two years. It's like being a captain of a ship, where the decisions made can steer the entire vessel towards success or failure.

Sofia: And finally, what about qualifications?

Me: Qualifications are the foundation of any role. You list the expected qualifications needed for the role, such as education, skills, and experience. Then, compare them to the actual qualifications of the role occupant. It's like ensuring that a builder has the right tools and expertise to construct a sturdy building. The right qualifications are essential for performing the job effectively.

Sofia: This is a comprehensive approach for defining the context. What about the competencies needed for the role?

Me: Our 3P Leadership Model and Prosperity Chakras help define the target competencies based on a progressive maturity scale. It's like setting up a ladder where each rung represents a higher level of maturity and skill. Employees are encouraged to self-assess and identify areas for improvement, guided by their desire to progress to the next level.

Sofia: Can you tell me more about the different types of competencies that are important in job roles?

Me: Absolutely, Sofia. Competencies can be grouped into three main categories: personal, professional, and people competencies. Each group has specific competencies that are crucial for performing a role effectively. Let's start by listing them out.

Sofia: Sounds good. What are the competencies under personal competencies?

Me: Personal competencies include self-management, living the values, empathy, relationship building, and walk-the-talk culture. These competencies help individuals manage themselves and their interactions with others effectively.

Sofia: And what about professional competencies?

Me: Professional competencies cover expertise or know-how, decision-making, result orientation, process orientation, and communication. These are essential for executing tasks and achieving organisational goals efficiently.

Sofia: Finally, what are the people competencies?

Me: People competencies focus on team building, fairness, development, certainty, and continuous learning. These competencies are crucial for managing and working with others to create a positive and productive work environment.

Sofia: Great. Let's dive deeper into personal competencies first.

Me: Sure!

1. Self-Management: This involves functioning effectively by exhibiting self-control and self-confidence, even under critical situations with extreme load. It's like being a calm captain steering the ship through a storm, thoroughly prepared for any challenge.

2. Living the Values: This means consistently demonstrating adherence to ethical values in both one-on-one and group interactions. Imagine it as being the moral compass of a team, guiding everyone towards ethical behaviour.

3. Empathy: Demonstrating humility and empathy involves understanding from another person's perspective and being open to changing your own perspective. It's like putting yourself in someone else's shoes to truly understand their journey.

4. Relationship Building: Developing effective working relationships and trust with colleagues by respecting others and maintaining a positive attitude. Think of it as cultivating a garden, where trust and respect are the seeds that grow into strong, lasting connections.

5. Walk-the-Talk Culture: Personally practising and advocating for a "walk-the-talk" culture, effectively addressing any issues observed consistently. It's like being a role model who not only talks about values but also lives by them every day.

Sofia: These personal competencies make a lot of sense. Can you explain the professional competencies now?

Me: Of course.

1. Know-how: Demonstrating expertise, especially in analysing and systematically solving problems, primarily in

one's own domain. This includes immediate containment actions, root cause analysis, and corrective and preventive actions, while respecting others' competence. It's like being a master craftsman who not only fixes issues but also prevents them from happening again.

2. Decision-Making: Demonstrating initiative and desire to lead, with analytical and transparent decision-making. This involves setting priorities based on facts and figures and validating gut feelings before concluding. Think of it as being a skilled chess player, making strategic moves based on careful analysis.

3. Result Orientation: Creating a result-oriented atmosphere by planning, setting goals, KRAs, KPIs, delegating, reviewing, and controlling effectively to establish accountability. It's like being a coach who ensures the team is focused, accountable, and achieves its goals on time.

4. Process Orientation: Demonstrating commitment and persuasion to meticulously follow and ensure that teams adhere to set standards and regulations without any deviations, achieving quality and cost excellence. It's like being a conductor who ensures every musician follows the score precisely to create a flawless performance.

5. Communication: Understanding top-down, bottom-up, and peer-to-peer communication needs and communicating effectively with clarity and commitment. This involves providing adequate objective and subjective content in a structured manner. Think of it as being a skilled diplomat who communicates clearly and effectively with everyone.

Sofia: I see. Now, what about the people competencies?

Me: Here they are.

1. Team Building: Creating relatedness and involvement through inclusive, cooperative approaches with peers, staff, and superiors for excellence in teamwork. It's like

being a builder who constructs a strong, cohesive team foundation.

2. Fairness: Creating a healthy working atmosphere by always demonstrating fair approaches and practices without bias or prejudice, preferably for avoiding and handling complaints and grievances. It's like being a judge who ensures fairness and justice in every situation.

3. Development: Investing time in managing and developing people individually and collectively by encouraging changes in inherent behaviour through appropriate feedback and coaching after delegating tasks. Think of it as being a gardener who nurtures each plant to grow to its full potential.

4. Certainty: Creating a sense of certainty by evolving and deploying inclusive strategies for fulfilling the organisation's mission and vision. This involves addressing purpose, agenda, recap, open points, actions (responsible/ timeline), feedback, minutes, and follow-up until validation in all interactions. It's like being a navigator who charts a clear course for the organisation to follow.

5. Learning: Creating a continuous improvement and learning-oriented environment by encouraging and managing change effectively while using failures as learning opportunities without any blame game. It's like being an explorer who constantly seeks new knowledge and learns from every experience.

Sofia: This is very comprehensive. How do these competencies come together in practice?

Me: Once the target attributes are defined, every role occupier is required to do a self-assessment. Then, an expert conducts an assessment in discussion with the role occupier, identifying development areas and setting clear expectations. It's like having a coach who helps athletes understand their strengths and areas for improvement, guiding them towards peak performance.

Sofia: This sounds like a robust system. What's the ultimate benefit of having such detailed job role descriptions?

Me: The ultimate benefit is creating a high-performance organisation where everyone knows their roles, responsibilities, and how they contribute to the overall success. It's like having a well-tuned orchestra where each musician knows their part, resulting in a harmonious and powerful performance. This clarity and structure lead to increased accountability, better collaboration, and a stronger, more resilient team.

Homework:

With whom do you want to share your insights on Job Role Description?

Who will be your accountability buddy for handholding and implementing your insights?

How have you described the roles you need for fulfilling your Key Performance Indicators and how are you using them to develop and enable the role occupants?

Creating and Implementing Standards

Creating and implementing standards in a business is vital for ensuring consistency, enabling meaningful comparisons, facilitating scaling up, and achieving execution excellence. Standards serve as a blueprint for operations, guaranteeing that every process is performed uniformly, which minimises errors and increases efficiency. They allow for benchmarking and performance measurement, helping to identify areas for improvement and fostering continuous growth. As businesses expand, standardised procedures make it easier to replicate successful models across new locations or divisions. Ultimately, robust standards drive execution excellence by aligning all team members with the organisation's goals and methods, ensuring that everyone is working towards the same high-quality outcomes.

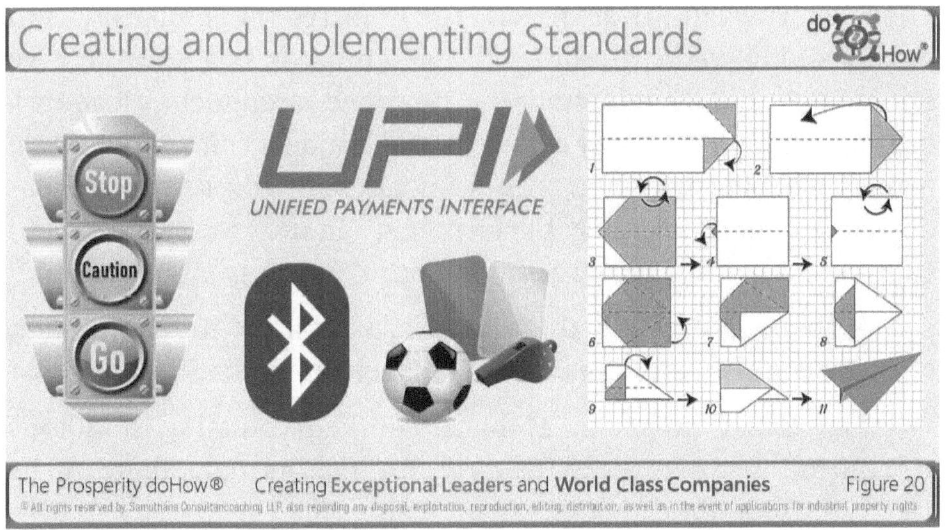

The Prosperity doHow® Creating Exceptional Leaders and World Class Companies Figure 20

Creating and implementing standards effectively is the key to prospering with the CORE, SUSTAIN, and ADVANCE.

Mohan, the new Chief Operating Officer (COO) of a large enterprise, is in his early 50s. He is impressed with the number of standards that have been created within the organisation he has recently joined but is simultaneously challenged by the very poor adherence to these standards.

Mohan: I've noticed that our company has an impressive array of standards in place, but adherence to them is surprisingly poor. What's your take on this?

Me: Let me start with a quote by Thomas A. Edison, "Genius is one percent inspiration and ninety-nine percent perspiration." I see that you have a challenge with the 99% perspiration, which I believe is like running a marathon, Mohan. We can also call it Excellence. It's not just about speed but also about endurance and continuous improvement. It involves maximising value and delivering exceptional customer experiences through well-defined standards that guide every step from inception to refinement.

Mohan: What do you mean by "standards"? How are they created?

Me: Think of standards as the rulebook for a game. They encapsulate best practices, industry benchmarks, and organisational goals. Creating these standards is a collaborative effort, like building a house. You need architects (leaders), engineers (subject matter experts), and builders (cross-functional teams) working together. The foundation involves setting clear objectives, defining key performance indicators (KPIs), and aligning everything with the overarching business strategy.

Mohan: In creating these standards you mentioned earlier, what are the critical success factors that ensure their effectiveness?

Me: Great question, Mohan. Think of creating standards as crafting a masterpiece. Several key factors contribute to its success, just like different elements coming together to create a beautiful painting.

Mohan: What would be the first factor in this masterpiece?

Me: Stakeholder involvement is crucial. It's like gathering a team of artists where everyone from leaders to frontline workers contributes their perspectives. This ensures the standards reflect diverse insights and needs, making them more robust and comprehensive.

Mohan: How do you ensure that these standards are well-integrated and coherent?

Me: Imagine building a puzzle. Each piece must fit seamlessly with the others. Similarly, standards need to be integrated and coherent, aligning with the organisation's overall strategy and processes. This coherence ensures that all parts of the organisation move in harmony towards common goals.

Mohan: What about benchmarking?

Me: Benchmarking is like having a map for our journey. By comparing our practices with industry bests, we set high standards and identify areas for improvement. It ensures that our standards are not just good but among the best, guiding us towards excellence.

Mohan: How do you keep these standards relevant and up-to-date?

Me: Think of standards as a living document, like a garden that needs regular tending. Keeping them relevant and up-to-date involves continuous review and adaptation to changing market trends, technologies, and customer needs. This dynamic approach ensures the standards remain effective and applicable.

Mohan: How can these standards be made practical and achievable?

Me: It's like setting realistic fitness goals. Standards need to be practical and achievable, meaning they should be realistic and within reach of the organisation. This ensures that everyone can follow them without feeling overwhelmed, leading to consistent application and success.

Mohan: How important is clarity in these standards?

Me: Clarity is paramount. Think of clear instructions for assembling furniture. If the standards are clear and unambiguous, everyone knows exactly what is expected, reducing confusion and errors. Clear standards are easier to implement and follow.

Mohan: And user-friendliness?

Me: User-friendliness is like having a handy toolkit. The standards should be easy to understand and apply. This ensures that employees can quickly refer to them and implement them effectively without needing extensive training or assistance.

Mohan: Flexibility sounds important too. How do you incorporate that?

Me: Absolutely. Flexibility is like having a versatile Swiss Army knife. Standards should be adaptable to different situations and capable of evolving with the organisation's needs. This flexibility ensures they remain relevant and useful in a dynamic environment.

Mohan: How do you ensure the standards are specific and measurable?

Me: Specific and measurable standards are like having clear milestones on a hiking trail. They provide precise targets and criteria for success, making it easier to track progress and measure outcomes. This specificity helps in assessing whether the standards are being met effectively.

Mohan: What about enforceability?

Me: Enforceability is like having traffic rules. Standards need to be enforceable and verifiable, meaning there should be mechanisms to monitor compliance and take corrective actions if necessary. This ensures that the standards are not just guidelines but are actively followed and maintained.

Mohan: How do you ensure quick closed-loop control?

Me: Quick closed-loop control is akin to having a responsive thermostat that adjusts the temperature in real-time. It involves setting up feedback mechanisms to quickly detect deviations and make necessary adjustments. This responsiveness ensures that standards are continuously met and improved.

Mohan: These success factors sound comprehensive. How do they come together in practice?

Me: Imagine an orchestra, Mohan. Each success factor is like a different instrument, and when they all play in harmony, they create beautiful music. By incorporating these factors, organisations can create effective, practical, and adaptable standards that drive excellence and continuous improvement. This holistic approach ensures that standards are not just theoretical but are actively contributing to the organisation's success.

Mohan: Once these standards are created, how do you ensure they are implemented effectively?

Me: Implementing standards is like orchestrating a symphony. It requires meticulous planning and strong leadership to ensure all the musicians (team members) play in harmony. Transparent communication is key; everyone must understand the "why" behind the new standards and the benefits they bring. Providing training and resources is like giving musicians the right instruments and music sheets. Realistic timelines and achievable milestones help in maintaining the rhythm and flow during the transition.

Mohan: How do you sustain these standards once they're in place?

Me: Sustaining standards is akin to maintaining a well-oiled machine. The standards must become part of the organisation's

DNA. Regular audits, performance reviews, and feedback loops act as routine maintenance checks. Recognising and rewarding employees who embody these standards is like lubricating the gears, ensuring smooth operation. Fostering a culture of continuous learning and improvement keeps the machine adaptable and efficient in the face of evolving challenges.

Mohan: Now that we've talked about implementing and sustaining standards, are there key factors in implementing and following them effectively too?

Me: Implementing and following standards is like planting and nurturing a tree. Various elements must come together harmoniously to ensure it grows strong and healthy. Let's dive into these factors.

Mohan: I remember service when you mention planting and nurturing. How does a service mindset play a role?

Me: A service mindset is like being a gardener who tends to the plants not just for their own sake but for the benefit of others. When team members adopt a service mindset, they follow the standards not just for themselves but to support their colleagues and the organisation. It is like following the traffic rules for others, isn't it? This mindset fosters a collaborative and supportive environment where everyone works together towards common goals.

Mohan: That's insightful. Does an aspirational purpose drive adherence to standards?

Me: Think of an aspirational purpose as the North Star that guides sailors. When people understand and believe in the higher purpose behind the standards, they are more motivated to adhere to them. This purpose provides a sense of direction and meaning, driving commitment and dedication to following the standards.

Mohan: What about involving people in preparing the standards, which we spoke about earlier?

Me: Involving people in preparing the standards is like having a community come together to build a playground. When team members contribute to the creation of standards, they feel a sense of ownership and are more likely to follow them. This involvement ensures the standards are practical, relevant, and reflective of the collective wisdom of the group.

Mohan: Yes, of course. How do you ensure the standards are easy to follow?

Me: The standards need to be like a well-designed user manual for a gadget—clear, concise, and easy to understand. They should be integrated into daily practices in a practical way, making it straightforward for everyone to follow without unnecessary complexity. This simplicity reduces barriers and increases compliance.

Mohan: Got it. I am not sure if our team is trained to meet our standards. How important is training in this process?

Me: Training is essential, much like teaching someone to ride a bike. Regular training and retraining ensure that everyone understands the standards and knows how to apply them correctly. It keeps everyone up-to-date and reinforces the importance of following the standards consistently.

Mohan: Absolutely! What do you do when challenges arise in following the standards?

Me: Handholding through challenges is like having a coach guide you through a difficult climb. Providing support and guidance when difficulties arise helps team members navigate obstacles and adhere to the standards. This support fosters a sense of confidence and capability.

Mohan: I noticed that we have a blame culture here. How does a no-blame culture contribute to this?

Me: A no-blame culture is like having a safe space where mistakes are seen as learning opportunities. Instead of pointing fingers, questions are asked to understand why the standard wasn't met and how it can be improved. This approach encourages openness and continuous improvement, making it easier for everyone to follow the standards without fear of retribution.

Mohan: These factors seem interrelated. How do they come together in practice?

Me: Imagine a symphony orchestra. Each factor is like a different instrument, and when they all play together harmoniously, they create beautiful music. By fostering a service mindset, grounding actions in an aspirational purpose, involving people in the creation process, designing easy-to-follow standards, providing ongoing training, offering support, and maintaining a no-blame culture, organisations can ensure effective implementation and adherence to standards. This holistic approach ensures that standards are not only created but are lived and breathed by everyone in the organisation, driving excellence and continuous improvement.

Mohan: What about continual improvement? How do you keep the standards relevant?

Me: Excellence is a never-ending journey, much like climbing a mountain. Regularly evaluating and improving standards ensures you keep ascending. Collecting and analysing data on process performance, customer satisfaction, and market trends helps identify areas needing enhancement. Collaborative problem-solving and brainstorming sessions are like finding new routes to tackle challenging terrains. Adapting standards to incorporate new technologies and methodologies is essential to maintain a competitive edge, much like updating your climbing gear.

Mohan: This has been incredibly insightful. I feel like I have a solid understanding of how to create and implement standards effectively.

Me: I'm glad to hear that, Mohan. Remember, implementing and following standards is like nurturing a garden—you need the right mix of planning, involvement, training, and a supportive culture to see it flourish.

Mohan: Absolutely. The analogies really helped me visualise how these success factors come together. I feel more confident about tackling my challenges now.

Me: That's wonderful to hear. By embracing these principles and fostering a culture that values continuous improvement and collaboration, you'll be well on your way to achieving excellence.

Mohan: Thanks so much for sharing your wisdom. I'm excited to start applying these insights.

Me: You're welcome, Mohan. Best of luck with your journey towards excellence. Remember, it's a continuous process, but with the right mindset and approach, you'll achieve great things.

Mohan: Thank you! I'm looking forward to it.

Homework:

With whom do you want to share your insights on Creating and Implementing Standards?

Who will be your accountability buddy for handholding and implementing your insights?

How have you ensured that anyone other than you can perform and deliver consistently with the same meticulousness, you would have done?

Business Process Excellence

The business process for routines is essential for ensuring consistency in delivering high-quality results through established good practices. By standardising routines, businesses can streamline operations, reduce errors, and enhance efficiency. This approach involves creating and following systematic procedures for regular tasks, which helps maintain a predictable and reliable performance. Consistent routines also provide a clear framework for employees, making it easier to train new staff and integrate them into the workflow. Moreover, standardised business processes facilitate continuous improvement, as they can be regularly reviewed and optimised based on feedback and changing needs. Implementing well-defined routines ensures that everyone in the organisation is aligned and working efficiently towards common goals.

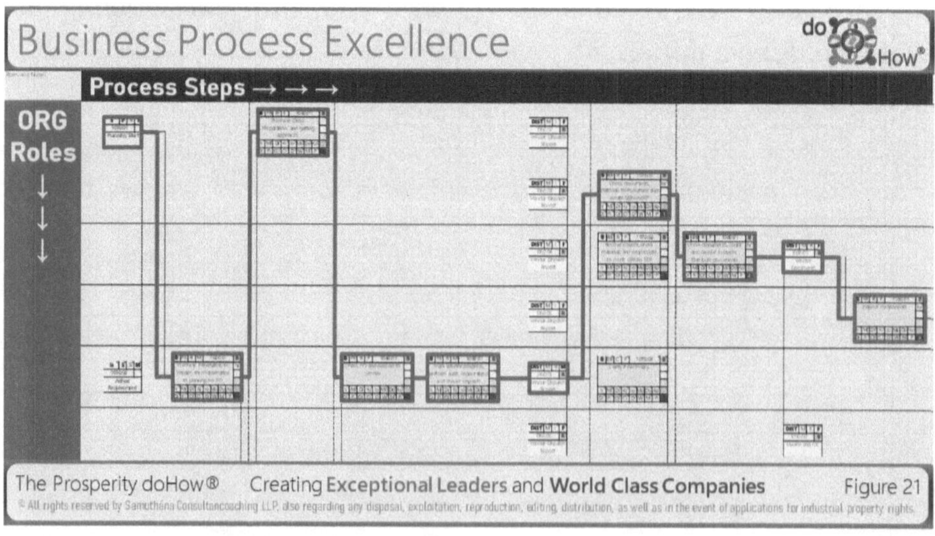

The Prosperity doHow®   Creating Exceptional Leaders and World Class Companies   Figure 21

Business process for routines ensures consistency in the CORE, SUSTAIN, and ADVANCE.

Introducing Hans, a sales executive in his late 20s, who is struggling to become effective in sales despite having many senior colleagues to learn from. Hans is eager to discuss how establishing a business process for routines can help him improve his sales performance.

Hans: Hi, I've been having a hard time becoming effective in sales, even though I have many experienced colleagues around me. I'd love to hear your thoughts on how establishing a business process for routines can help me.

Me: Sure, Hans! Imagine business process management as the backbone of an efficient organisation. It's like a well-choreographed dance where every step is precise and purposeful. Business process management ensures that every action in an organisation is well-documented, efficient, and aimed at achieving specific outcomes.

Hans: When you say well-choreographed dance, I am sure you mean that these are tried and tested steps. Correct?

Me: Absolutely. Hans, it's crucial to focus on standardising and documenting business processes that consistently deliver favourable outcomes because it ensures we are capturing, replicating, and scaling best practices in use. This targeted approach helps avoid the creation of procedures just for the sake of formality, which can lead to bureaucratic inefficiencies and stifle innovation.

Hans: Oh! Yes! I see where you are going. Business process management must enable instead of being a deterrent. Correct?

Me: Certainly. By documenting only successful business processes, we promote a culture of excellence where each documented business process has a proven track record of adding value, enhancing quality, and achieving strategic objectives. This not only optimises resources but also empowers employees by providing clear, actionable guidelines rooted in success, ultimately leading to sustained organisational growth and performance.

Hans: That sounds crucial. How do we start with business process management?

Me: We begin with context setting, much like setting the stage for a performance. This involves understanding the current business processes, seating teams to leverage diverse perspectives, and introducing the basics of business process management. Think of it as getting everyone on the same page before the main event starts.

Hans: Interesting. What are the key elements in describing a business process?

Me: Great question! When describing a business process, it's like writing a story. We start with numbering for easy navigation, a telegraphic title for clarity, and a brief purpose to set the scene. Just as a book has chapters, business processes have steps, each with a top-level business process and possibly next-level business processes. This structure ensures that everyone understands the flow and importance of each step.

Hans: How do you decide the importance of each business process?

Me: Think of it like prioritising tasks in a to-do list. We categorise business processes based on their impact on product quality, timelines, and costs. High-impact business processes are like the main plot points in a story, while medium and low-impact business processes are the subplots and details that support the main narrative.

Hans: Who is responsible for these business processes?

Me: Just like a director and producer in a film, we have business process sponsors and owners. The sponsor, often a senior executive, ensures the business process is implemented effectively. The owner, usually at the working level, documents and maintains the business process, making sure it runs smoothly.

Hans: What about the hierarchy in business process management?

Me: Picture a pyramid. At the top, we have the management manual, which outlines the purpose and key outcomes. The next-level details cross-functional business processes that span multiple departments. Below that are functional business processes within specific roles, and at the base are workplace instructions and standard operating procedures. This hierarchy ensures clarity and accountability at every level.

Hans: How do we identify the stakeholders in a business process?

Me: Stakeholders are like the audience and critics of our performance. We identify customers and their expectations, suppliers and their competencies, and internal roles with the necessary qualifications. If multiple roles overlap, we define each role clearly to avoid confusion and ensure smooth operation.

Hans: That makes sense. What about collecting business process time data? How does that fit into this?

Me: Collecting business process time data is vital for understanding and improving efficiency. We look at metrics such as Turn-Around-Time (TAT) in hours, Touch Time in minutes, the percentage of queries, and Clarification Time in days. This data provides insights into where delays or inefficiencies might be occurring and helps us streamline business processes. It's like having a stopwatch for each step, allowing us to see exactly where time is spent and how we can optimise it.

Hans: How are business process steps detailed?

Me: Detailing business process steps is like choreographing a dance. We number the steps, give them clear titles, and describe their purpose. We classify them into production, business, projects, or time-out steps. Each step includes details like necessary equipment, roles involved, and triggers to start and end the step, ensuring every move is precise and synchronised.

Hans: And what about the roles within these business process steps? How do we ensure everyone knows their responsibilities?

Me: Defining business process roles clearly is essential for accountability and smooth operation. We have specific roles like the Responsible Role, which is the Driver Role, ensuring the business process moves forward. The Approval Role is where the "buck stops," providing final decisions and oversight. Collaborating Roles are active participants who work directly on tasks, while Support Roles are passive participants who assist as needed. Finally, Information Recipients are those who need a "heads-up" on the business process status but aren't directly involved. By clearly nominating people to these roles, we ensure everyone knows their responsibilities and can collaborate effectively.

Hans: How do we measure the success of these business processes?

Me: Metrics are our scorecards. We define key performance indicators (KPIs) to monitor the effectiveness and efficiency of business processes. It's like tracking a player's performance in a game. We have KPIs for outcome validation and resource utilisation, and we ensure these are monitored regularly. This helps us stay on track and make necessary adjustments.

Hans: What do you mean regularly?

Me: We set specific intervals—daily, weekly, monthly, quarterly, or yearly—for monitoring, reporting, and reviewing the different key performance indicators (KPIs). This ensures timely updates and allows us to steer the business process effectively. The Responsible Role typically handles this, ensuring metrics are reported on time. We use real-time dashboards to provide instant access to these metrics and review meeting proceedings for quick reference. This is like having regular check-ins in a project to ensure everything is on track and any issues are addressed promptly.

Hans: What about training and auditing?

Me: Training is like rehearsals before the main show. We communicate and train everyone involved, using methods like classroom sessions, on-the-job training, or e-learning. Audits are our reviews and feedback sessions. We have checklists, set audit frequencies, and ensure any non-conformance is immediately addressed with corrective actions.

Hans: And Kaizen?

Me: Ah, Kaizen is the philosophy of continuous improvement. It's like refining a performance with every show. We capture improvement opportunities, track their status, and implement changes. This ongoing business process helps us stay agile and continuously enhance our efficiency and effectiveness.

Hans: Wow, Me, this really paints a clear picture. Business process management sounds like a dynamic and structured approach to achieving excellence.

Me: Exactly, Hans. It's all about creating a seamless, efficient, and continuously improving organisation, just like a well-directed and evolving performance.

Homework:

With whom do you want to share your insights on Business Process Excellence?

Who will be your accountability buddy for handholding and implementing your insights?

How are you repeating the routines and activities that delivered consistent performance?

Project for Tasks

The concept of "Project for Tasks" is crucial for achieving consistency in creating transformations within a business. This approach involves organising and managing tasks as part of larger, well-defined projects to ensure systematic progress and tangible results. By treating each task as a component of a broader project, businesses can maintain focus, prioritise effectively, and allocate resources efficiently. This method facilitates clear goal setting, detailed planning, and continuous monitoring, which are essential for delivering high-quality outcomes on time. Projects for tasks help in breaking down complex objectives into manageable steps, ensuring that each phase of transformation is executed with precision and consistency. This structured approach not only enhances delivery performance but also drives continuous

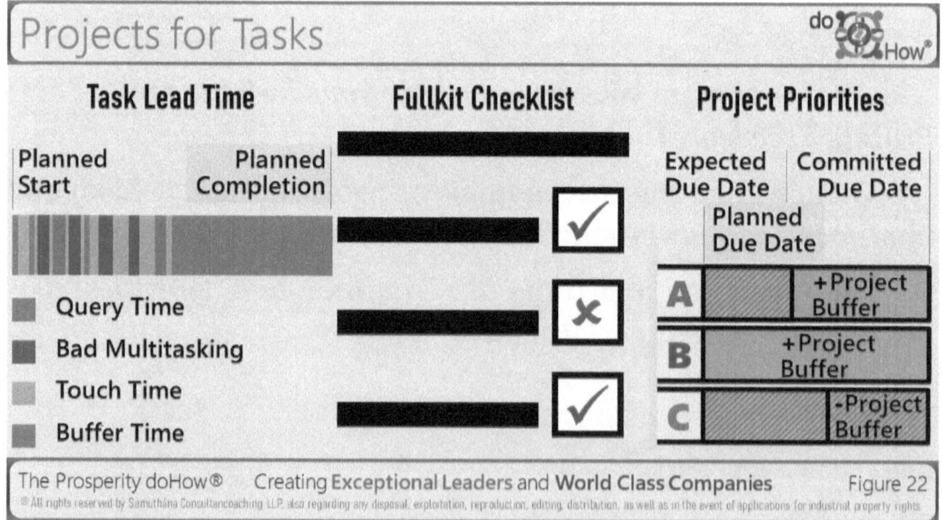

improvement and innovation, leading to sustained business growth.

Projects for tasks ensure effective fulfilment of KPIs in the CORE, SUSTAIN, and ADVANCE.

Introducing Tom, a business head in a capital goods company in his late 40s, who is keen to significantly improve delivery performance. Tom is interested in understanding how adopting a "Project for Tasks" approach can help him achieve better results and drive transformations within his organisation.

Tom: Hi, I'm looking to significantly improve our delivery performance. I've heard about the "Project for Tasks" approach and would love to hear your thoughts on how it can help us achieve more consistent transformations.

Me: Good evening, Tom! I'm doing well, thank you. Today, let's dive into the fascinating world of projects and task management.

Tom: Great! Why are projects so interesting to you?

Me: Projects are interesting because everything is new in them. Unlike operations, where tasks are repetitive and predictable, projects involve unique challenges and outcomes. It's like venturing into unknown territory each time. If it wasn't unique, it would just be operations.

Tom: What are the fundamental differences between operations and projects?

Me: That's a great question. When I was implementing manufacturing technology development in Germany between 2000 and 2006, and later in Italy with Thomas Group Consultants, I learnt a lot about this. In operations, you have functions like planning, production, quality control, maintenance, and sales. These functions are repetitive and consistent. In projects, you have similar functions, but they are often named differently and involve unique challenges.

Tom: Can you give an example of how these functions differ?

Me: Sure. In operations, the quality function ensures products meet specifications and there are no deviations. In projects, this function is called risk management because the focus is on managing uncertainties and ensuring the project meets the desired outcome despite the unknowns. Similarly, product development in operations is often called design in projects. The key difference is that projects involve unique, one-time tasks, while operations involve repetitive tasks.

Tom: So, projects are all about dealing with uncertainty?

Me: Exactly. In projects, you're often doing something for the first time and the last time, which brings a high level of uncertainty. This uncertainty requires a different mindset. Planning in projects isn't just about following a set path; it's about anticipating surprises and adapting to them. It's like sailing in uncharted waters where you need to be ready for unexpected storms.

Tom: How do you manage this uncertainty?

Me: One effective way is by using buffers. In projects, we don't assign buffers to individual tasks because we can't predict where delays will occur. Instead, we place a contingency buffer at the end of the project timeline. This way, if any task takes longer than expected, it eats into the project buffer, not the individual task's buffer. It's like having an emergency fund for unexpected expenses.

Tom: That makes sense. How do you track progress in a project?

Me: Tracking progress involves regular updates on the expected completion date and the percentage of work remaining for each task. It's like having a daily health check-up. We use a scoreboard to quickly understand the current status, discuss successes and failures from the previous day, and review the rolling plan for the next few days. This ensures everyone is aligned and any issues are addressed promptly.

Tom: What about the roles within a project? How do you ensure everyone knows their responsibilities?

Me: Defining roles in a project is crucial for accountability and effective collaboration. We have specific roles like the Responsible Role (Driver Role), Approval Role ("Buck Stops Here"), Collaborating Roles (Active Role), Support Roles (Passive Role), and Information Recipients ("Heads-up"). Clearly defining these roles ensures accountability and smooth operation. It's like casting actors in a play, where each one knows their part to ensure a seamless performance.

Tom: How do you manage the budget and timelines in a project?

Me: Budget and timelines are managed by regularly updating the scoreboard with the latest data on expected completion dates, percentage of work remaining, and any changes to the project scope. We also monitor the project buffer to ensure we stay on track. It's like adjusting the sails and course of a ship based on the current conditions to ensure we reach our destination on time and within budget.

Tom: What about managing changes in the project scope?

Me: Managing scope changes is crucial. We accept that changes will happen and focus on understanding their impact on timelines and budgets. It's like being prepared for course corrections when sailing. Regular updates and open communication help us adapt and keep the project on track.

Tom: This sounds like a comprehensive approach. How do you ensure that everyone stays on the same page?

Me: Consistent and systematic reviews are key. Daily reviews help us stay updated on the project's status, address any issues, and make necessary adjustments. It's like having a daily huddle in sports to ensure the team is synchronised and ready to tackle the day's challenges. Regular recognitions and celebrations also help maintain high morale and reinforce positive behaviour.

Tom: This has been really insightful. It seems like a lot of thought and planning go into effective project management.

Me: Absolutely, Tom. Effective project management is about balancing meticulous planning with the flexibility to adapt to surprises. By focusing on successful processes, collecting time data, defining roles, setting clock speeds, and maintaining a positive mindset, we can create a seamless, efficient, and continuously improving organisation. It's like directing a dynamic and evolving performance where every role is clear, every action adds value, and every metric is closely monitored to ensure success.

Tom: I've heard you mention "full kitting" before. Can you explain what that is and why it's important?

Me: Absolutely, Tom. Full kitting is like preparing a meal. Imagine you're about to cook a complex dish; you gather all the ingredients, tools, and recipes you need before you start cooking. In the context of projects, full kitting means ensuring that all necessary resources—information, materials, decisions, standards, and documents—are available before starting a task. This preparation helps prevent delays and ensures smoother execution.

Tom: How does full kitting impact the efficiency of a project?

Me: Full kitting significantly boosts efficiency. Without it, you might start a task only to find halfway through that you're missing a critical component, forcing you to pause and scramble to find it. This is like starting to bake a cake and realising you don't have any eggs. Full kitting ensures that once you start, you can continue without interruptions. It's about being proactive and prepared, which reduces downtime and keeps the project on track.

Tom: Can you share an example where full kitting made a significant difference?

Me: Sure! In 2019, we introduced full-kit checklists at a global MNC struggling with project delays. They were dealing with turnkey EPC installations, where each project was unique.

By implementing start and completion full-kit checklists, we ensured that every task owner had everything they needed before starting and handed over a complete package to the next person. This approach transformed their project completion rates, and that year, they achieved their best record in history. It was like a relay race where each runner had everything they needed to run their leg efficiently.

Tom: That's impressive. How do you ensure that these checklists are followed consistently?

Me: Consistency comes from regular updates and reviews. We use mobile platforms for real-time status updates on the full-kit checklists. Task owners report the current status, including what's completed and what's pending. This visibility allows project coordinators to prioritise and address issues quickly. It's like having a project management dashboard that everyone can access to see the latest updates and progress.

Tom: I was thinking about how queries and multitasking affect our projects. Can you explain their impact?

Me: Of course, Tom! Imagine you're a juggler. Each query you run in a project is like tossing a ball into the air. When you run a query, you're looking for specific information, and just like a ball, you need to catch it to make use of it. Now, if you're juggling too many balls at once—each one representing a different task or query—it becomes harder to manage.

Tom: That's an interesting metaphor. So, what's the problem with juggling too many balls?

Me: Great question. When you juggle too many balls, your focus gets divided. Similarly, in a project, bad multitasking can lead to a drop in the quality of work because your attention is spread thin. Imagine trying to read a book while also having a conversation. You might miss key details in the book, and the conversation might not flow as smoothly.

Tom: Stop! What is bad multitasking? I am hearing for the first time.

Me: Bad multitasking is trying to multitask tasks and jobs that require conscious effort, like negotiating with your boss on a call using headphones about timelines and, at the same time, trying to pay a bill with UPI from your mobile. You will surely mess up one of the two. On the other hand, subconscious multitasking such as walking and listening to music. You can do both easily, right?

Tom: I see. So, now, let's get back to how the queries fit into this juggling act.

Me: Queries are like specific tasks you need to perform to get information or results. If you think of each project as a puzzle, queries are the individual pieces you need to find and fit together. The more queries you have to handle simultaneously, the harder it is to see the big picture. It's like trying to complete multiple puzzles at the same time without mixing up the pieces.

Tom: That sounds complicated. What happens if we don't manage our queries and multitask well?

Me: If queries aren't managed well, it can lead to a backlog, like having too many balls in the air that you can't catch. This can slow down the project's progress and even cause errors. For example, if you're working on a report and also trying to debug a piece of code, you might end up making mistakes in both because your mind keeps switching gears.

Tom: That makes sense. How can we manage this better?

Me: One way is to prioritise tasks and queries, like focusing on one ball at a time until you've mastered it before adding another. Think of it like cooking a meal. You wouldn't start all the dishes at once. Instead, you might prep the ingredients first, start cooking the main dish, and while it's simmering, work on the sides. By the time everything is ready, it's all perfectly timed.

Tom: So, it's about pacing and focus, right?

Me: Exactly! It's about finding a rhythm. For queries, this means running them in a sequence that makes sense for the project's goals and timeline. For bad multitasking, it means focusing on high-priority tasks first and grouping similar tasks together. It's like organising a toolbox. If you keep all related tools together, you can find and use them quickly without wasting time searching.

Tom: I get it now. It's like being a conductor of an orchestra, making sure each instrument comes in at the right time to create a harmonious performance.

Me: Perfect analogy, Tom! By managing queries and bad multitasking effectively, we can ensure each part of the project contributes to a successful outcome, just like each instrument contributes to a beautiful symphony.

Tom: This has been really insightful. It seems like a lot of thought and planning go into effective project management.

Me: Absolutely, Tom. Effective project management is about balancing meticulous planning with the flexibility to adapt to surprises. By focusing on successful processes, collecting time data, defining roles, setting clock speeds, ensuring full kitting, and maintaining a positive mindset, we create a seamless, efficient, and continuously improving organisation. It's like directing a dynamic and evolving performance where every role is clear, every action adds value, and every metric is closely monitored to ensure success.

Tom: Thanks, this really paints a clear picture of how to manage projects effectively.

Me: You're welcome, Tom. It's all about creating a well-directed and evolving performance. With the right mindset and tools, we can navigate the uncertainties of projects and achieve excellence.

Homework:

With whom do you want to share your insights on Projects for Tasks?

Who will be your accountability buddy for handholding and implementing your insights?

How are you replicating the tasks and actions that delivered consistent performance?

Continuous Manufacturing Flow

Continuous manufacturing flow is a crucial concept in production that focuses on the optimal usage of resources to add maximum value to customers. This approach involves designing and maintaining a seamless, uninterrupted production process where materials and products move smoothly from one stage to the next without delays or bottlenecks. By minimising downtime and eliminating waste, continuous manufacturing flow ensures that resources such as labour, machinery, and materials are used efficiently, reducing costs and improving overall productivity. This method not only enhances the quality and consistency of the final product but also boosts customer satisfaction by ensuring timely delivery and responsiveness to market demands. Implementing a continuous flow in manufacturing is essential for

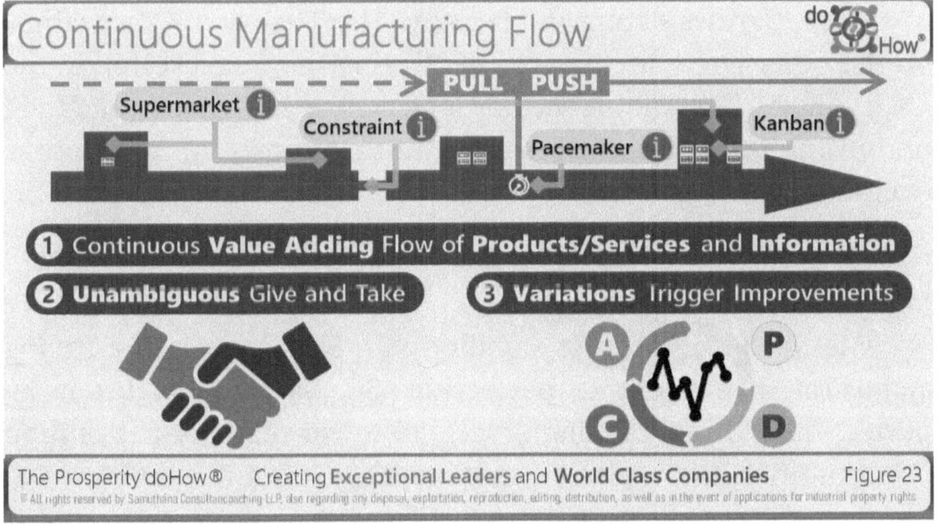

businesses aiming to remain competitive and responsive in today's fast-paced environment.

Continuous manufacturing flow is the foundation for enabling the CORE, SUSTAIN, and ADVANCE.

Introducing Ram, a production engineer in his late 20s, who is currently frustrated with frequent jams in the production line and the resulting wastage of resources. Ram is eager to discuss how continuous manufacturing flow can help address these issues and improve the efficiency of the production process.

Ram: Hi, I've been really irritated with the constant jams in our production line and the waste of resources. Can you explain how continuous manufacturing flow can help solve these problems?

Me: Good evening, Ram! Absolutely, continuous manufacturing flow is like a well-oiled machine where every part works seamlessly with the others. Let's dive into it.

Ram: Let's start with the basics. What is Lean Manufacturing and the Theory of Constraints?

Me: Lean Manufacturing is all about eliminating waste and ensuring every step in the manufacturing process adds value. Think of it like trimming a tree—removing unnecessary branches to ensure it grows strong and healthy. The Theory of Constraints, on the other hand, focuses on identifying the weakest link in the chain—much like finding the bottleneck in an hourglass—and then optimising the entire process around that constraint to improve overall performance.

Ram: How do you ensure process stability with Six Sigma capability?

Me: Ensuring process stability with Six Sigma is like tuning a musical instrument to perfection. Six Sigma aims for near-perfect quality by reducing defects to fewer than 3.4 per million opportunities. It can also be expressed as $Cp \geq 2.0$ and $Cpk \geq 1.5$.

It uses data-driven techniques to identify and eliminate variations, ensuring that the process is stable and predictable.

Ram: What about cycle time stability? How do you keep the variation less than 10%?

Me: Imagine a metronome ticking steadily. Keeping cycle time variation less than 10% means each manufacturing cycle happens consistently, like the ticking of that metronome. This consistency is achieved through rigorous monitoring and control, ensuring that every cycle is as close to the ideal as possible.

Ram: I've heard quick changeover is important. How does it work?

Me: Quick changeover is like a pit stop in a Formula 1 race. The goal is to minimise downtime by preparing as much as possible before the changeover begins—this is known as maximising external setup. Tools, parts, and materials are prepped in advance so the actual changeover happens swiftly and efficiently.

Ram: What is the role of a pacemaker in a manufacturing line?

Me: The pacemaker is the heartbeat of the manufacturing line, setting the pace for the entire process. It's the nodal point where flow is regulated to ensure that production meets demand without overproducing or creating bottlenecks.

Ram: How do you manage the flow of materials and products in this system?

Me: It's a dance of pulling and pushing. We pull upstream raw materials, components, and subassemblies—much like pulling ingredients to a chef's table just in time for cooking. Downstream, we push assemblies and finished products to ensure a steady flow to customers.

Ram: How do you prevent a constraint from starving in the process?

Me: Maintaining a buffer before a constraint is like ensuring a steady stream of water to a dam. This buffer prevents the constraint from running dry, ensuring it always has work to process, which keeps the entire line moving smoothly.

Ram: What are supermarkets in manufacturing, and how do they work?

Me: Supermarkets in manufacturing are like stocked shelves in a grocery store. They hold variants, subassemblies, and assemblies ready to be pulled as needed. This system keeps inventory at optimal levels and ensures that parts are available without overstocking.

Ram: Can you explain Kanban and its role in pulling materials?

Me: Kanban is like a traffic signal for materials. It signals when to pull raw materials, components, subassemblies, and assemblies from the supermarket. This visual cue ensures that inventory is replenished just in time, keeping the flow smooth and efficient.

Ram: How do you continually reduce waste, unevenness, and overburden?

Me: Reducing Muda (waste), Mura (unevenness), and Muri (overburden) is like weeding a garden. We constantly look for and eliminate anything that doesn't add value (DOWNTIME: Defect, Overproduction, Waiting, Non-Utilised Talent, Transportation, Inventory, Motion, Extra Processing). This continuous improvement ensures the garden—our manufacturing process—stays healthy and productive. Mura can be reduced by what is called levelling, wherein the production is planned at a constant rate as per a pre-established repeating pattern. Muri can be reduced by realistically calculating the capacity and planned based on realistic assumptions.

Ram: How do you maximise output from the constraint?

Me: Maximising output from the constraint is like tuning a bottleneck in a busy highway. We ensure that this point operates at maximum efficiency to increase overall throughput, which often involves optimising processes and resources around it.

Ram: What does it mean to subordinate decisions to the constraint?

Me: Subordinating decisions to the constraint means aligning every decision to support the constraint, like a coach planning a strategy around their star player. Every action taken is designed to ensure the constraint operates at its best, enhancing overall performance.

Ram: How do you elevate the constraint?

Me: Elevating the constraint is like upgrading a narrow bridge on a busy road. We invest in improving the capacity and efficiency of the constraint, which might involve new technology, additional resources, or process improvements to handle higher loads.

Ram: What about continually improving Overall Equipment Effectiveness (OEE)?

Me: Improving OEE is like fine-tuning a race car. We look at availability, performance, and quality metrics to ensure equipment is running at peak efficiency. Continuous monitoring and improvements help us squeeze out the maximum possible productivity from our equipment.

Ram: How do you improve the productivity of workmen with engineering solutions?

Me: Enhancing workmen productivity with engineering solutions is like giving athletes the best training and equipment. We provide tools, ergonomic setups, and efficient workflows that reduce strain and increase efficiency, ensuring workers can perform at their best.

Ram: What is the importance of a clear handshake between giver and taker?

Me: A clear handshake between giver and taker is like a relay race baton pass. It ensures smooth transitions and clear communication, so the next person knows exactly what to do, minimising confusion and delays.

Ram: How do you minimise variations by focusing on outliers?

Me: Minimising variations by focusing on outliers is like adjusting the tuning of a guitar string that's slightly off-key. By identifying and addressing the anomalies, we bring the entire process into harmony, ensuring consistent quality and performance.

Ram: Thanks for the wonderful explanation from the system perspective. Can you tell me about the role and importance of people in this process?

Me: Of course. People are absolutely central to maintaining and improving continuous manufacturing flow. Think of them as the conductors of an orchestra, ensuring that every instrument plays in harmony to create a beautiful symphony.

Ram: Interesting analogy! But how exactly do people contribute to this process?

Me: Well, let's break it down. First, we have the operators on the shop floor. They are like skilled musicians, each playing their part with precision. They ensure that machines run smoothly, perform quality checks, and quickly address any issues that arise. Their expertise and attention to detail are crucial for maintaining the flow of production.

Ram: So they're the ones directly handling the production. What about the managers and supervisors?

Me: Managers and supervisors are akin to the orchestra's conductor. They oversee the entire process, ensuring that everything runs smoothly and efficiently. They coordinate the different sections, manage resources, and make decisions that keep the production line moving. They also play a critical role in identifying bottlenecks and implementing solutions to improve efficiency.

Ram: It sounds like communication is key here. How do they ensure effective communication?

Me: Absolutely, communication is vital. It's like the conductor's baton guiding the musicians. Clear and consistent communication ensures that everyone knows their roles and responsibilities, understands the production goals, and is aware of any changes or issues that arise. Regular meetings, daily stand-ups, and real-time updates through digital dashboards help maintain this communication flow.

Ram: What about the role of continuous improvement? How do people contribute to that?

Me: Continuous improvement is where the magic happens. It's like fine-tuning an instrument to achieve perfect pitch. Employees at all levels are encouraged to identify areas for improvement and suggest changes. This can involve anything from tweaking a machine's settings to redesigning a workflow for better efficiency. This culture of continuous improvement relies on the creativity and problem-solving skills of the people involved.

Ram: How do you ensure that everyone is on board with continuous improvement?

Me: It's about fostering a culture where everyone feels valued and heard. Think of it like a jazz band where each musician has the opportunity to improvise and contribute to the overall performance. Encouraging open dialogue, recognising contributions, and providing training and development opportunities are essential. When people feel that their ideas are valued, they are more likely to take ownership and actively participate in continuous improvement.

Ram: Can you give me an example of how people-driven improvements have made a difference?

Me: Sure! In one company, operators noticed that a particular machine setup was causing frequent delays. They suggested a minor adjustment in the workflow, which reduced setup time by 20%. This change, driven by the people on the ground, led to a significant increase in overall efficiency. It's like discovering a shortcut in a complex piece of music that makes the performance smoother and more enjoyable.

Ram: That's impressive. How do you maintain this momentum and ensure continuous engagement?

Me: Maintaining momentum is like keeping the rhythm in a dance. Regular feedback loops, celebrating successes, and continuous training are key. Leaders need to stay engaged and show genuine interest in the ideas and well-being of their teams. When people see that their efforts lead to tangible improvements and are appreciated, they remain motivated to keep pushing for excellence.

Ram: So, it sounds like people are not just cogs in the machine but the driving force behind continuous manufacturing flow.

Me: Exactly, Ram. People are the heart and soul of the process. Their skills, insights, and dedication are what keep the machinery running smoothly and the improvements coming. Just like an orchestra can't create beautiful music without its musicians, a manufacturing process can't achieve continuous flow without its people.

Ram: This has been incredibly enlightening. Thanks for explaining the crucial role of people as well in continuous manufacturing flow so clearly!

Me: You're welcome, Ram! Remember, at the end of the day, it's the people who bring the system to life and drive it towards greater efficiency and innovation. Continuous manufacturing flow is all about creating a smooth, efficient, and adaptable process. With the right mindset and tools, we can achieve remarkable consistency and productivity.

With whom do you want to share your insights on Continuous Manufacturing Flow?

Who will be your accountability buddy for handholding and implementing your insights?

How are you making sure that your products seamlessly flow in your value stream?

Execution Planning

Execution planning is critical for ensuring that business goals are met despite unforeseen hurdles. This approach involves meticulously outlining the steps needed to achieve objectives, considering potential risks, and developing contingency plans. Effective execution planning ensures that teams are prepared to handle unexpected challenges without derailing progress. It includes allocating resources, setting timelines, and defining roles and responsibilities clearly. By anticipating potential obstacles and having strategies in place to address them, businesses can maintain momentum and achieve their targets more reliably. Execution planning not only enhances operational efficiency but also builds resilience, enabling organisations to adapt and thrive in the face of uncertainty.

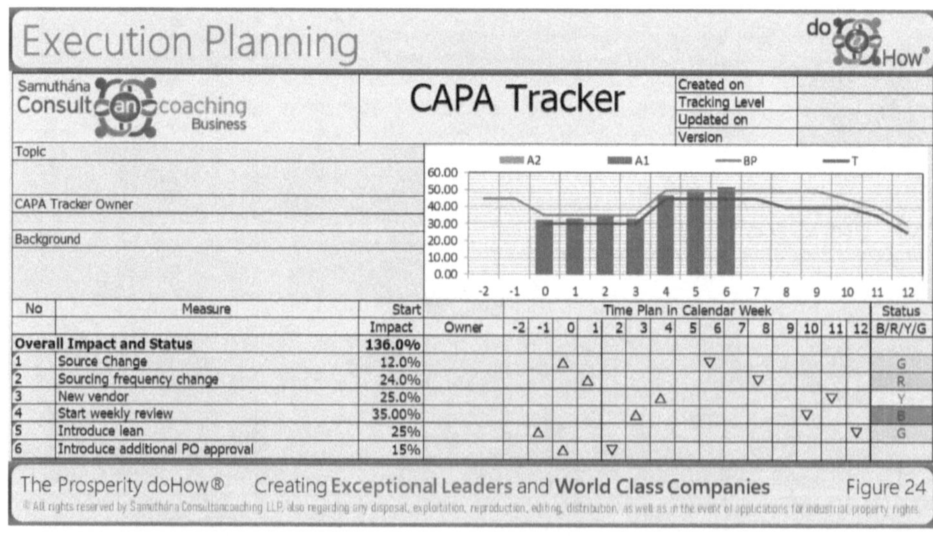

Execution Planning — do How®

Samuthána Consult**can**coaching Business

CAPA Tracker

Created on	
Tracking Level	
Updated on	
Version	

Topic

CAPA Tracker Owner

Background

No	Measure	Start		-2	-1	0	1	2	3	4	5	6	7	8	9	10	11	12	Status
		Impact	Owner	-2	-1	0	1	2	3	4	5	6	7	8	9	10	11	12	B/R/Y/G
	Overall Impact and Status	**136.0%**																	
1	Source Change	12.0%				△						▽							G
2	Sourcing frequency change	24.0%					△					▽							R
3	New vendor	25.0%							△							▽			Y
4	Start weekly review	35.00%							△						▽				B
5	Introduce lean	25%			△												▽		G
6	Introduce additional PO approval	15%					△	▽											

Execution planning is the human intelligence behind the successful implementation of the CORE, SUSTAIN, and ADVANCE.

Introducing Ivan, a supply chain director in his mid-40s, who is frustrated with team members missing out on inventory targets. Ivan is keen to discuss how execution planning can help improve performance and ensure targets are consistently met.

Ivan: Hi, I've been really frustrated with my team missing inventory targets. I'm interested in understanding how execution planning can help us overcome these issues. What are your thoughts?

Me: Absolutely, Ivan. Execution planning is like setting a GPS for a road trip. You need to know where you are starting from, understand the current road conditions, and then plan your route. If you base your plan on assumptions, like wishing the traffic will be light without checking, you might end up in a jam.

Ivan: That makes sense. So, how should one start planning for execution?

Me: Start by preparing detailed plans for different time frames: tomorrow, next week, next month, next quarter, and even next year. Imagine these as checkpoints on your journey. Each step should align with your ultimate goal, like stops on the way to your final destination.

Ivan: What if unexpected events occur along the way? How do we account for those?

Me: Always aim to achieve at least 20% more than your goal to account for unforeseen surprises. Think of it as packing extra snacks for your trip, just in case you get hungry or stuck somewhere.

Ivan: And if the goal is quite large, how should we break it down?

Me: Break down the goal into smaller, manageable sub-goals. It's like dividing a long journey into several legs. Each sub-goal acts as a rest stop, giving you a clear path and milestones to celebrate along the way.

Ivan: What about specific actions needed to achieve the goal?

Me: List out one-time actions necessary for achieving the goal, including start and end timelines, who is responsible, and how much they will contribute to the goal. It's like scheduling pit stops to refuel and check your vehicle's health during your journey.

Ivan: And for ongoing tasks?

Me: Identify all necessary routines, detailing who is responsible, the evidence of completion, frequency (daily, weekly, etc.), and when to start. These routines are like your car maintenance checks—regular and essential for a smooth ride. Ensure these routines and actions together contribute at least 120% of your goal.

Ivan: Why aim for 120%?

Me: Aiming for 120% ensures you have a buffer. Think of it as carrying an extra spare tyre; it's better to have it and not need it than to need it and not have it.

Ivan: How do we handle timelines and potential delays?

Me: Define targets based on your clock speed, with a buffer for delays. If you plan to reach a destination in five hours, tell yourself it might take six, accounting for possible traffic.

Ivan: What if we realise we can't meet the goal on time?

Me: Re-evaluate your plan. Add more actions and routines to ensure you can still hit the 120% target. It's like finding alternate routes or speeding up where possible if you're running behind schedule.

Ivan: How do we ensure everything stays on track?

Me: Automate follow-ups to ensure tasks are completed. Regularly update actual achievements against the goal and adjust forecasts if needed. It's like keeping your GPS updated with real-time traffic data to adjust your route if necessary.

Ivan: What if things don't go as planned?

Me: Review what went well and what didn't. Learn from these experiences to make your next plan more realistic. It's like reflecting on your road trip to plan better for the next one, knowing where the construction zones were and where you found the best coffee stops.

Ivan: How important is success as a motivator in this process?

Me: Success is like the fuel that keeps your car running. When you see progress, even in small increments, it boosts your morale and keeps you motivated. Realistic planning is crucial because it sets achievable milestones. Each success, no matter how small, is a checkpoint that reassures you that you're on the right track. It's like seeing the distance to your destination getting shorter and shorter on your GPS—each mile passed is a success that drives you forward.

Ivan: Can you explain how success in realistic planning impacts motivation?

Me: Think of it this way: if you set out to drive 1,000 miles and all you focus on is the final destination, the journey can feel overwhelming. But if you break it down and celebrate each milestone—100 miles, 200 miles, and so on—you're constantly reminded of your progress. This makes the journey feel manageable and keeps your spirits high. Success breeds confidence. When you achieve realistic sub-goals, it builds momentum, making the next leg of the journey feel more attainable. It's like climbing a mountain; reaching each base camp gives you the energy and confidence to tackle the next stage.

Ivan: How do we make sure our plans are both realistic and ambitious?

Me: That's a great point, Ivan. It's vital to thoroughly understand both the current reality and our untapped potential. This understanding is like knowing your car's current fuel level and its full tank capacity. Realistic planning must be grounded in what is actually possible right now, while still stretching to better utilise our full capabilities. This stretch is like pushing your car to get the best mileage out of a full tank while being mindful of fuel efficiency.

Ivan: How do we identify our untapped capabilities?

Me: Look for areas where there is potential for improvement or untapped resources. It's like finding shortcuts or more efficient routes that you haven't tried before. Understanding and leveraging these can significantly enhance your planning. For example, if you realise your team can handle more tasks with better tools or training, incorporate that into your plan. It's about maximising what you have while being realistic about the journey.

Ivan: That makes sense. How do we balance this understanding with setting ambitious goals?

Me: Balance comes from setting goals that push the boundaries of your current capabilities while staying grounded in reality. It's like setting a challenging yet achievable distance for a day's drive based on your car's performance and road conditions. Stretch goals should motivate you to push harder but not be so far-fetched that they become discouraging. It's about knowing your limits and pushing them a bit further each time.

Ivan: Why is execution planning all about succeeding against all odds?

Me: Execution planning is about preparing for the journey and succeeding despite challenges. It's like setting out on an adventure where you might face unexpected detours or obstacles. The essence of execution planning is to anticipate these hurdles, plan with contingencies, and stay adaptable. Success in this context means achieving your goals even when the odds are stacked against you. It's about resilience, determination, and the ability to navigate through uncertainties with a clear, realistic, and adaptable plan. It's like being a skilled navigator who can read the stars and the compass, adjusting the sails to reach the destination despite storms and calm seas alike.

Homework:

With whom do you want to share your insights on Execution Planning?

Who will be your accountability buddy for handholding and implementing your insights?

How are you planning to succeed against all odds and consistently meet your goals?

Regular Reporting

Regular reporting is a vital practice in business that ensures all team members can effectively prioritise their tasks and align their efforts with organisational goals. By providing consistent updates on performance metrics, progress, and any issues, regular reporting creates transparency and keeps everyone informed. This practice helps in identifying areas that need attention, making timely decisions, and adjusting strategies as needed. It enables team members to understand how their work contributes to the larger objectives, fostering a sense of accountability and motivation. Regular reporting also facilitates communication and collaboration, ensuring that everyone is on the same page and working towards common goals. Overall, it enhances efficiency, supports informed decision-making, and drives continuous improvement.

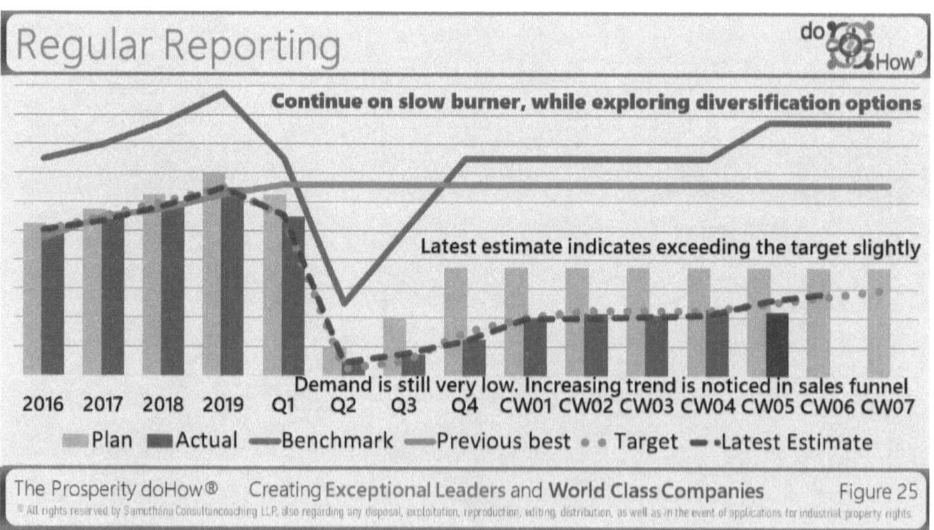

Regular reporting enables informed decision-making in the CORE, SUSTAIN, and ADVANCE.

Introducing Klaus, an operations manager in his late 30s, who spends a significant amount of time understanding daily performance levels. Klaus is eager to explore how regular reporting can streamline his efforts and improve the overall efficiency of his team.

Klaus: Hi, I spend a lot of time trying to understand our daily performance levels. I'm curious about how regular reporting can help streamline this process. What are your thoughts?

Me: Absolutely, Klaus. Reporting is crucial for keeping everyone informed and on track. Think of it like telling a story—each level adds more depth and detail. Let's start with the five levels of reporting.

Klaus: Sounds interesting. What's the first level about?

Me: Level 1 is all about immediate and honest reporting when a job is completed. It's like a student handing in their homework as soon as they finish, making sure they explain what they did and why they did it, covering the 5 W's and 2 H's—why, who, what, when, where, how, and how much. At this level, you report when asked and keep everything straightforward.

Klaus: What changes in Level 2?

Me: At Level 2, you add a bit more awareness. It's like a student not only turning in homework but also understanding the cost of materials used and seeking feedback for improvement. You use the reporting time to understand your superior's thinking and apologise for any errors. You also consider the other party's circumstances, showing empathy and readiness to act on mistakes.

Klaus: How about Level 3?

Me: Level 3 introduces "interim reports." Imagine a student working on a long-term project. They don't wait until the end to give updates; they provide progress reports when situations change or when they reach certain milestones. Here, you clearly define objectives, understand the importance of content and method, and prepare reference materials.

Klaus: What's added at Level 4?

Me: Level 4 is where you start to add your own opinions and proposals. Think of it as a student not only reporting on their project status but also analysing what's working and what's not, then suggesting improvements. You report your analysis, propose corrective actions, and share pertinent efforts with superiors, subordinates, and related departments.

Klaus: And finally, Level 5?

Me: Level 5 is the pinnacle. It's like a student who not only delivers a comprehensive project report but also anticipates what the teacher wants to see and provides even more than expected. You report in the manner desired by the other party and take responsibility if communication fails. This level is about going beyond expectations and understanding what others seek.

Klaus: That's a great structure. Are there specific tips to make reporting even more effective?

Me: Definitely! These tips will help ensure your reports are insightful and actionable. Let's go through them one by one.

Klaus: Sure, let's start with the first tip.

Me: The first tip is about understanding past performance trends. It's like looking at a series of past report cards to see how a student has progressed. Knowing where you've been helps you understand where you're going. This trend helps in setting the foundation for your current situation.

Klaus: And the second tip?

Me: After understanding the past, the next step is to assess the actual latest performance. Think of it as checking the most recent test score to see if the trend continues. This helps in confirming if things are moving as expected or if there's a deviation that needs attention.

Klaus: What comes next?

Me: The third tip is about recognising the best-validated performance. This serves as a benchmark, like knowing the highest score ever achieved in a subject. It helps assess the already exploited potential and sets a standard for future performance.

Klaus: How do we use comparisons?

Me: A like-to-like comparison benchmark is crucial. It's important to compare apples to apples, like comparing scores from the same class or subject to uncover hidden potential. This gives a fair assessment of performance relative to similar contexts.

Klaus: How about targets?

Me: The fifth tip is using the target defined in agreement to assess actual performance. It's like aiming for a specific grade and checking if you've met it. Having a clear target provides direction and purpose, making it easier to measure success.

Klaus: And the expected outcomes?

Me: The expected yield from the plan is essential. This tip is about understanding what you expected to achieve, like predicting grades based on study hours. It helps in assessing how realistic your plan is and what adjustments might be needed.

Klaus: What if the situation changes?

Me: That brings us to the seventh tip, which is about making the latest estimate based on reality. This is like estimating your final grade based on current performance trends. It's crucial for maintaining a culture of predictability and adapting to changes.

Klaus: What if there's a gap between estimates and targets?

Me: The eighth tip is explaining the gap to the target. It's like understanding why you might be falling short of your desired grade. This explanation adds value to the report by highlighting areas for improvement and understanding the reasons behind any shortfalls.

Klaus: What about analysing the current situation?

Me: The ninth tip is to analyse the current situation considering chances and risks. It's like reflecting on study habits and exam preparation to understand what's working and what's not. This deep dive helps in identifying opportunities and threats that might affect outcomes.

Klaus: Finally, what about summarising everything?

Me: The last tip is to provide a summary with recommendations. It's like a student summarising their study plan and next steps to improve their grades. This summary helps in assessing the overall situation and empowers decision-makers with clear, actionable insights.

Klaus: That's a thorough approach. So, it's not just about reporting what happened but also understanding and anticipating what needs to be done next.

Me: Exactly, Klaus. Regular reporting isn't just about checking boxes; it's about storytelling with data, anticipating needs, and planning for success. It's about succeeding against all odds, much like navigating through a challenging course and still aiming to excel. By understanding and implementing these levels and tips, we can ensure our reporting is not only comprehensive and insightful but also geared towards continuous improvement and success.

Homework:

With whom do you want to share your insights on Regular Reporting?

Who will be your accountability buddy for handholding and implementing your insights?

How do you know in real-time the progress made by all your team members and the challenges that they may be facing?

Regular Steering

Regular steering is an essential practice in business that focuses on overcoming execution challenges and ensuring that projects and operations stay on track. This involves periodic meetings and reviews where teams assess progress, identify obstacles, and make necessary adjustments to plans. The primary purpose of regular steering is to maintain alignment with strategic goals, address issues promptly, and keep the momentum going. By continuously monitoring and steering the course of action, organisations can adapt to changes, optimise performance, and ensure that targets are met efficiently. This practice fosters accountability, enhances communication, and supports a proactive approach to problem-solving, ultimately driving better outcomes and continuous improvement.

Regular steering overcomes challenges through coordinated improvisation in the CORE, SUSTAIN, and ADVANCE.

Introducing João, a management trainee in a large company in his mid-20s, who often wonders why meetings seem so useless. João is interested in understanding how regular steering can make meetings more productive and effective in overcoming execution challenges.

João: Hi, I often find myself wondering why so many of our meetings seem useless. Can you explain how regular steering can actually make a difference and help overcome execution challenges?

Me: Absolutely, João. Let's talk about why many people think meetings are useless before we discuss routine steering meetings.

João: That's a good place to start. Why do people feel that way?

Me: People often see meetings as timewasters because they've experienced poorly managed ones. It's like being stuck in traffic with no clear signs or directions—you're just wasting time. Many meetings lack a clear agenda, drag on without purpose, and end without actionable outcomes. Participants leave feeling like they've gained nothing and just lost precious time.

João: That does sound frustrating. So, what makes a meeting effective and efficient?

Me: Effective and efficient routine steering meetings are the backbone of successful companies. They're like a well-planned road trip where everyone knows the destination, the route, and their role in getting there. When structured properly, meetings provide direction, facilitate coordination, and ensure that everyone is aligned and moving towards the same goals.

João: How do structured meetings contribute to success?

Me: Think of structured meetings as the steering wheel of a car. Just like you need to constantly steer and adjust your direction while driving, especially in city traffic, regular meetings help you navigate through business challenges. Without them, you're like a driver cruising on a motorway without any direction, which can be disastrous when unexpected obstacles arise.

João: Interesting analogy. So, how does this apply to companies?

Me: Many companies avoid structured meetings, seeing them as a waste of time or an unwelcome accountability check. It's like athletes who don't huddle or strategise during a game—they end up uncoordinated and likely to lose. Companies need these meetings to set ambitious goals and steer through obstacles efficiently. Otherwise, they end up with mediocre outcomes due to a lack of direction and synchronisation.

João: Can you break down the different types of steering meetings and their success factors?

Me: Sure! Let's start with the Daily Stand-up Meeting/Huddle.

João: What makes daily stand-ups effective?

Me: Daily stand-ups are like a morning warm-up routine. They cover essential metrics like innovation, productivity, quality, cost, delivery, response time, safety, and morale. You analyse the successes and failures of the previous day and make adjustments for today. Think of it as a football team reviewing yesterday's game and planning today's strategy.

João: How do you keep the team focused during these huddles?

Me: We use tools like a Rolling Plan or a Task Kanban to prioritise tasks and ensure everyone knows their roles and goals. It's like a well-oiled machine where each part works in harmony. Immediate issues are addressed on the spot, and any non-conformities are managed through containment decisions. Recognising and celebrating successes also keeps the team motivated and inspired.

João: What role do scorecards and dashboards play in these meetings?

Me: Updated scorecards, dashboards, or cockpit charts are essential. They act like the instrument panel in a car, providing real-time data on key performance indicators. Without them, you're driving blind. These tools help track progress, identify issues quickly, and make data-driven decisions.

João: What about the Weekly Sharpening Meeting?

Me: Weekly meetings are like a pit stop in a race. You check if the daily stand-ups are consistent and effective. Open points and actions are reviewed, and deviations from the previous week are prioritised for learning. It's a deeper dive than daily huddles, much like a mechanic checking the car's engine, not just the fuel level.

João: How do you handle deviations in these meetings?

Me: We perform root cause analyses to understand why deviations occurred and plan corrective and preventive actions. It's about being proactive, like anticipating and fixing potential issues in a car before they become major problems. This also includes updating standards and procedures to prevent future issues.

João: And the Monthly Management Meeting?

Me: Monthly meetings are like a comprehensive health check-up. The agenda is set in advance, and everyone comes prepared. We validate the effectiveness of daily and weekly meetings and review stakeholder and business scoreboards. It's like looking at an athlete's overall performance metrics—trends, benchmarks, and best performances.

João: What do you discuss in these meetings?

Me: We discuss customer, shareholder, employee, vendor, and societal satisfaction. We also check agile maturity, system audits, and process effectiveness. Individual presentations lead to clear decisions and budget changes to ensure smooth operations until the next meeting. It's a strategic discussion, like a coach planning the season's playbook.

João: How important are updated dashboards and scorecards in these meetings?

Me: They're crucial. Think of them as your game stats—knowing your strengths and weaknesses helps you strategise better. Up-to-date dashboards provide a snapshot of the current business health and highlight areas needing attention. They ensure everyone has the same understanding and can make informed decisions.

João: Finally, what happens in the Quarterly Board Meeting?

Me: Quarterly meetings are like an annual sports awards ceremony combined with a strategy session. We visit the Gemba (workplace) to interact with people, distribute awards, and review financial statements. This meeting involves reviewing the business's overall health, strategic direction, compliance, and governance. Detailed discussions lead to strategic decisions and approvals for the next quarter's business plan, including CAPEX projects. We review the company's mission, vision, and long-term plans. The minutes clearly demarcate items for information, comments to consider, and actions to be taken. It's about setting a clear, actionable path forward, much like a team setting goals for the next season.

João: What about the yearly meetings?

Me: They start and end the annual cycle focused mainly on purpose and strategy. They are like the annual maintenance and overhauling breaks in power plants when the entire power plant gets refurbished and upgraded. In essence, these retreats are vital for keeping the light of leadership and management bright and effective, ensuring that the organisation navigates smoothly towards its goals.

João: All these meetings appear to be cyclic, don't they?

Me: Absolutely correct. The Learning to Learn System was the first concept I introduced to my mentoring clients based on my experience with such cycles working seamlessly in Bosch.

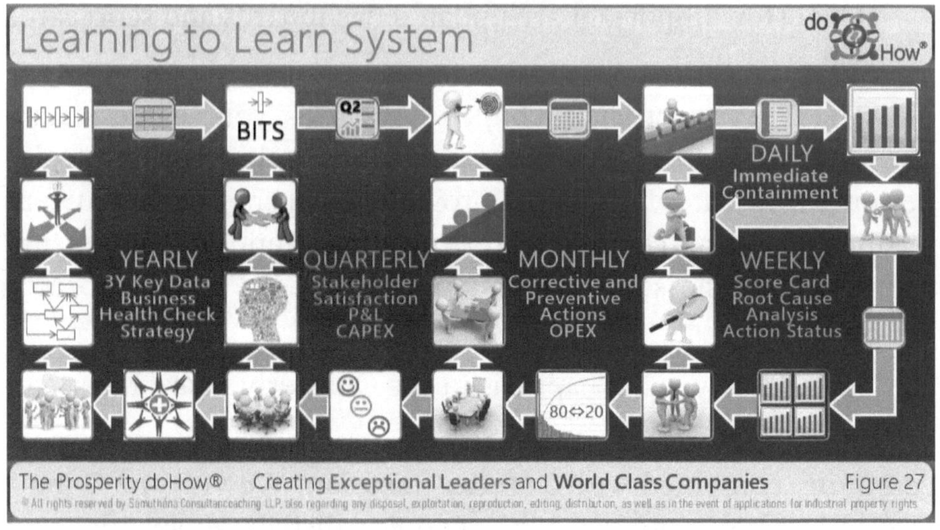

The Prosperity doHow®   Creating Exceptional Leaders and World Class Companies   Figure 27

João: How do you ensure these meetings are productive?

Me: Let me start by mentioning that meetings are the heartbeat of our collaboration, where ideas converge and strategies are born. To make our meetings efficient and effective, we commit to being purposeful with our time, present in our engagement, and proactive in our contributions. By preparing thoughtfully, listening actively, and focusing on clear outcomes, we transform our gatherings into powerful catalysts for progress. Together, we can create a culture of respect and productivity that not only drives our success but also honours each individual's valuable time and talents.

João: It seems like regular meetings are not just about checking in but steering the company towards success.

Me: Exactly, João. These meetings ensure everyone is aligned, motivated, and ready to tackle challenges head-on. They're about succeeding against all odds, much like a determined team winning despite tough competition. Regular, structured reviews ignite the spark needed to achieve amazing outcomes. By incorporating routine steering meetings, updated scorecards, dashboards, and cockpit charts, companies can ensure continuous improvement, alignment, and motivation, leading to extraordinary achievements even in the face of challenges.

Homework:

With whom do you want to share your insights on Regular Steering?

Who will be your accountability buddy for handholding and implementing your insights?

How are you ensuring that your entire team is on the same page regarding the improvisations necessary to meet the goals?

Problem-Solving

Problem-solving is a critical function in any business, aimed at identifying, addressing, and eliminating issues to ensure smooth operations and prevent recurrence. Effective problem-solving involves a systematic approach to diagnosing the root cause of a problem, developing and implementing solutions, and monitoring the results to ensure the issue is resolved permanently. This process not only "kills" the problem but also puts measures in place to prevent it from happening again. By fostering a proactive problem-solving culture, businesses can enhance their efficiency, reduce downtime, and improve overall quality and performance. It encourages continuous improvement and innovation as teams learn from each challenge and develop better practices over time.

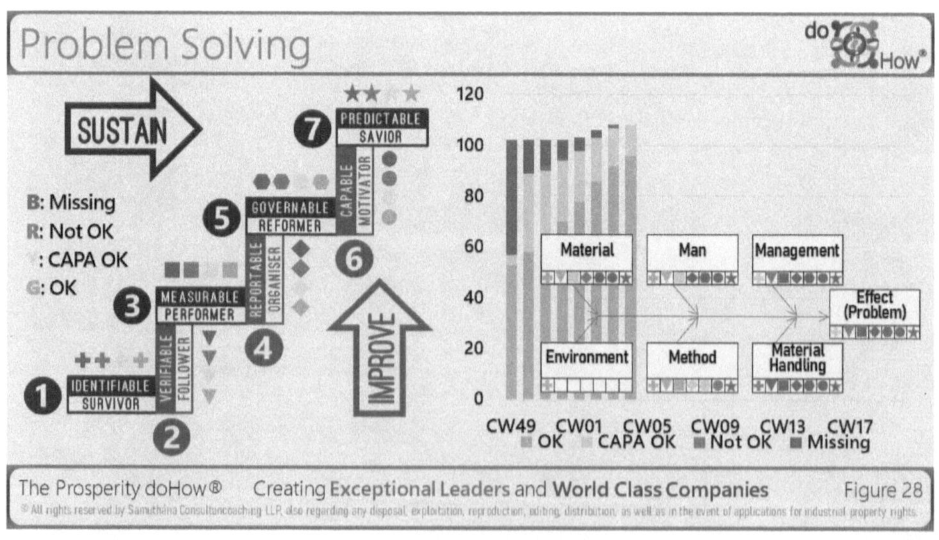

Problem-solving provides a platform for sustainable progress in the CORE, SUSTAIN, and ADVANCE.

Introducing Anna, a quality assurance executive in her late 30s, who is very disturbed by continuously recurring problems in her work. Anna is eager to discuss how effective problem-solving strategies can help her eliminate these issues and improve her team's performance.

Anna: Hi, I'm really disturbed by the continuous recurrence of problems in my work. Can you explain how effective problem-solving strategies can help eliminate these issues for good? What is DMAIC, that I have heard so often?

Me: Sure, Anna. Think of DMAIC as a structured method for solving problems. It's simple in theory but can seem complex in practice. For those who are natural problem solvers, it's intuitive. For others, it might feel like trying to read Greek and Latin. But let's break it down step by step so it becomes clearer.

Anna: That sounds good. But before we dive into DMAIC, how do you define a problem in a business context?

Me: A problem in business is when the actual outcome doesn't meet the expectations. Problem-solving is about narrowing down the problem, determining the root cause, and implementing corrective and preventive actions to ensure the solution is sustainable. It's like fixing a leaky roof—you need to narrow down and find where the leak is, understand why it's happening, fix it, and then take steps to prevent future leaks.

Anna: You mentioned the importance of narrowing down the problem in problem-solving. How exactly do you do that? What questions should we ask?

Me: Great question, Anna. Narrowing down the problem is like being a detective. You need to gather clues to get to the root of the issue. Let's dive into the key questions you should ask. Each question helps peel back a layer, much like peeling an onion, to get to the core of the problem.

Anna: So, where do we start?

Me: Start by asking, who is impacted and who is not? Imagine you're trying to find out why certain plants in a garden are wilting while others are thriving. Identifying which plants are affected helps you understand the scope of the problem. Look for any noticeable changes over time. Are there differences in soil, water, or sunlight between the affected and unaffected plants?

Anna: That makes sense. What's next?

Me: Next, ask what is happening and what could have happened but has not. It's like comparing a healthy plant to a wilting one. What symptoms are present in the wilting plant that aren't in the healthy one? This helps highlight what's going wrong and what should be happening instead. Notice any changes over time, like how the wilting progressed or if the healthy plant showed signs of the same issue previously.

Anna: I see. And how about the location aspect?

Me: Then, ask where it is happening and where it could have happened but hasn't. Picture different sections of a garden. If one area is thriving while another is struggling, you need to explore why. Is it a matter of soil quality, exposure to elements, or perhaps pests? Differences in location can provide vital clues about the underlying causes.

Anna: How do you consider the timing of the problem?

Me: Timing is crucial. Ask when it is happening and when it could have happened but hasn't. This is like noticing that a plant wanes more during certain times of the day. Understanding the timing can reveal patterns and triggers. Has the problem appeared suddenly, or has it been gradually developing? Are there specific times when the issue is more pronounced?

Anna: What about the magnitude of the problem?

Me: Finally, consider the magnitude by asking what the observed magnitude is and what could have been the magnitude but is not. Think of this as measuring how severe the wilting is. Is it just a few leaves, or is the entire plant affected? Comparing the observed severity with what could potentially happen helps assess the extent of the problem and its possible impact.

Anna: So, by asking these questions, we can narrow down the problem effectively?

Me: Exactly, Anna. Each question helps you gather pieces of the puzzle. It's like being an investigator, carefully examining clues and patterns to solve a mystery. By understanding who is impacted, what is happening, where it's happening, when it's happening, and the magnitude, you can get a clearer picture of the problem. This thorough examination allows you to target your efforts precisely and find the most effective solutions.

Anna: This is really insightful. Can you summarise the key to narrowing down a problem?

Me: Sure. Think of it like a detective's investigation. You start broad by identifying who is affected and then narrow down by examining what is happening, where it's occurring, the timing, and the magnitude. Each question helps you peel back a layer, revealing more about the core issue. This methodical approach ensures you don't overlook any vital clues and allows you to address the problem comprehensively and effectively. Once this is done, we can dive into the key steps of problem-solving.

Anna: So, what are the key steps in problem-solving?

Me: Let's start with Define. The key to defining a problem is to truly understand it. Imagine trying to fix a car without looking under the hood. You need to visit the location where the problem is happening to see, feel, and understand the reality firsthand. Communication often gets distorted, so seeing the problem directly is crucial. It's like feeling the vibe of a place; you can't describe it unless you're there.

Anna: How do you narrow down the problem once you've seen it?

Me: You need to stratify the problem by asking critical questions like, where is it occurring? Where is it not occurring? When does it happen? And how much does it affect things? This helps break down the problem into more manageable parts. Think of it as peeling an onion layer by layer to get to the core. Also, ensure that the problem is genuine and not just perceived. Sometimes, issues are created for recognition or other reasons. Verify the problem before diving into solving it, much like verifying if the symptoms you feel are really due to a cold or something else.

Anna: What about the Measure phase?

Me: Measurement is about quantifying the problem. The first success factor is standardisation—making sure everyone measures the same way. It's like using a standard recipe in cooking; everyone should use the same measurements for consistent results. You also need to ensure the accuracy of your measurements, like using a precise thermometer instead of guessing the temperature. The frequency of measurement is crucial too. It depends on the nature of the problem. If it's a production issue, you might measure hourly. For strategic issues, weekly might suffice. The idea is to match the clock speed to the problem. It's like checking your car's fuel level more frequently on a long trip compared to a short one.

Anna: Let's move on to the Analyse phase. What happens here?

Me: Analysing involves identifying the root cause of the problem. Create a cause-and-effect diagram, also known as an Ishikawa or fishbone diagram. This helps visualise the potential causes of a problem. It's like mapping out all possible reasons why a plant isn't growing well—poor soil, lack of water, insufficient sunlight, etc. Look for correlations between different variables using statistical tools to see if changes in one factor affect another. It's like connecting the dots to see the bigger picture. Once you identify potential causes, validate them by testing—like changing one variable at a time and observing the effects.

Anna: What's next after analysis?

Me: The Improve phase is where you implement solutions. You start with containment actions to prevent the problem from worsening. Then, introduce corrective and preventive actions based on your analysis. It's like treating a patient: first, stabilise them, then address the root cause to prevent future issues. Validate the improvements by monitoring their impact over time. Ask why the defect occurred, why it wasn't detected earlier, and why it wasn't predicted. It's like making sure the medicine is working and the patient isn't just temporarily feeling better.

Anna: Finally, what about the Control phase?

Me: Control is about sustaining the improvements. Implement systems to ensure the problem doesn't recur. This might involve regular audits, automated reporting, or built-in checks. It's like setting up a health monitoring system to ensure the patient stays healthy long-term. Control measures should be clear and unambiguous, ensuring the problem is eliminated and doesn't reoccur.

Anna: That's very detailed. How does problem-solving integrate with regular assessments and reviews?

Me: Problem-solving is continuous. I use a flow assessment approach to regularly validate and improve processes. It's about consistency and common sense—always checking if practices meet expectations, identifying top contributors to problems, and taking focused actions. Think of it as a gardener regularly tending to plants to ensure they thrive. Let me explain how I approach problem-solving.

Anna: Sure, go ahead.

Me: First, segment and focus. Imagine you have a garden with some plants thriving and others struggling. Start by identifying the top contributor to the problem, much like focusing on the most troubled plant. Dive deep into understanding what's affecting that particular plant before moving on to the next. This method helps narrow down the problem and allows for targeted actions. It's like isolating the issue to find the best solution.

Anna: And what about the actual review process?

Me: Instead of long workshops, I use weekly reviews. These are short, focused meetings that define actions for the top contributing segment and cause. It's like having a weekly check-up on your plants to see if the fertiliser is working or if the watering schedule needs adjustment. This keeps the team focused and ensures actions are taken promptly. It's about maintaining momentum and making continuous progress.

Anna: How do you maintain consistency in this process?

Me: Consistency is key. Regularly validate the effectiveness of solutions and ensure they are sustainable. Think of it as routine checks and balances to keep the process on track. It's like consistently checking the health of your plants, ensuring they get the right nutrients and care. This involves routine evaluations to see if the solutions are holding up over time and making adjustments as needed.

Anna: How do you ensure the solutions are sustainable?

Me: By using maturity levels to assess processes. We look at how well a practice is followed, verified, measured, reported, governed, and improved over time. Let's break down these levels. But before that, we need to create a cause-and-effect diagram.

Anna: I've heard about cause-and-effect diagrams, but I'm not entirely sure how they work. Can you explain them to me?

Me: Of course, Anna. A cause-and-effect diagram, also known as a fishbone or Ishikawa diagram, is a tool used to identify, explore, and visually display the possible causes of a specific problem. Think of it as a roadmap that helps you trace back from an issue to its root causes.

Anna: Why is it called a fishbone diagram?

Me: Good question! It's called a fishbone diagram because its structure resembles the skeleton of a fish. The problem or effect is the head of the fish, and the main causes are like the spines branching off the backbone. Each main cause can then have sub-causes branching off further. It visually organises potential causes in a way that makes it easier to see relationships and pinpoint the root of the problem.

Anna: That's interesting. How do you start creating one?

Me: Start by clearly defining the problem. This is the "head" of the fish. For example, if a car isn't starting, the problem statement might be "Car won't start." Once you have the problem defined, draw a horizontal line to represent the "spine" of the fish.

Anna: Okay, and what's next?

Me: Next, identify the main categories of potential causes. These are the "bones" that branch off the spine. For our car example, the main categories might include "Engine," "Battery," "Fuel System," and "Ignition System." These categories help organise the causes into broader areas to investigate.

Anna: How do you find the specific causes within those categories?

Me: This is where you start brainstorming. Under each main category, list possible specific causes. For example, under "Battery," you might have "Battery dead," "Battery connections loose," or "Alternator not charging battery." It's like playing detective—each potential cause is a clue that helps you narrow down the true issue.

Anna: What if you end up with a lot of potential causes?

Me: That's quite common, and it's part of the process. Think of it like peeling back layers of an onion. You start broad and then dig deeper. For each potential cause, you can ask further "why" questions. For example, if "Battery dead" is a cause, ask, "Why is the battery dead?" It might lead to "Alternator not working" or "Battery old and needs replacement." Before trying to identify the root cause, I recommend identifying the level of each of the potential causes. Shall I proceed?

Anna: Please do.

Me: The first level is Identifiable (Survivor). At this stage, the flow is regularly practised and can be clearly identified. It's like looking at a map of a city and being able to locate the origin and destination. Even if there are some interruptions, you can see the flow. It's essential for sustainability because you need to know where you're starting and where you're going.

Anna: The next level is verifiable, correct?

Me: Yes. Next is Verifiable (Follower). The flow can be easily verified by comparing it with a documented standard. It's like using a route map to a destination, which you can use to compare the actual position. This ensures you're on the right path and can make adjustments as needed. It's necessary for improvement because you have a standard to refer to.

Anna: Measurable next, correct?

Me: Yes. Then we have Measurable (Performer). The performance of the flow can be measured. It's like having a GPS device to measure the actual location. You have clear metrics to gauge how well things are working. This level is essential for sustainability because you need to track your progress accurately.

Reportable (Organiser) comes next. The performance is reported regularly on time for reviewing. It's like Google Maps regularly reporting traffic status and ETA. Regular updates help track progress and identify any issues promptly. This level is necessary for improvement because it keeps everyone informed and engaged.

Anna: What next?

Me: Governable (Reformer) follows. The performance is monitored, controlled, steered, and governed for stability. It's like checking road blockages ahead and deciding to take a deviation to reach the destination on time. Control mechanisms are in place to keep the process stable. This level is crucial for sustainability because it ensures the process runs smoothly and issues are addressed proactively.

Anna: So now we are in control. That's it?

Me: No. Still two to go. At the Capable (Motivator) level, the performance consistently meets targets and specifications. It's like confirming that the actual time of arrival was the same as or earlier than the estimated time of arrival. Your processes are reliable and consistently deliver the desired results. This level is necessary for improvement because it demonstrates that the system works effectively.

Anna: Oh! I see. Does anything come after capable?

Me: Oh yes. Finally, we reach Predictable (Saviour). The performance is predicted for taking preventive measures. It's like Google Maps maintaining the same ETA despite changes in traffic. You can foresee potential issues and take steps to prevent them, ensuring smooth operations. This level is essential for sustainability because it ensures long-term success by anticipating and mitigating risks.

Anna: How do you know which cause is the actual root cause, after identifying the levels for each of the potential causes?

Me: The goal is to drill down until you reach the most specific and actionable root cause. Often, you'll need to test your hypotheses. In our car example, you might test the battery and alternator to see which one is failing. It's like following a trail of breadcrumbs until you find the source of the problem.

Anna: So, the cause-and-effect diagram, including the levels, helps organise your thinking and investigation?

Me: Exactly! It provides a structured way to explore potential causes and see how they might be interconnected. It's like having a map that shows all possible paths leading to the problem, making it easier to decide which paths to investigate first. By systematically working through the diagram, you can methodically rule out causes and hone in on the true root of the issue.

Anna: That makes a lot of sense. How do you use this diagram once you've identified the root cause?

Me: Once you've identified the root cause, the diagram helps you plan your corrective actions. You can see all the contributing factors, which makes it easier to develop a comprehensive solution. It's like seeing the full picture and understanding how all the pieces fit together, allowing you to address the problem effectively and prevent it from recurring. The levels of the other causes help in dominating them and killing the problem.

Anna: This sounds like a powerful tool. Can it be used in different industries?

Me: Absolutely! The cause-and-effect diagram, as well as the levels, are versatile and can be used in any industry—from manufacturing and healthcare to education and service industries. Anywhere there's a problem that needs solving, this tool can help. It's like having a universal toolkit that adapts to any situation.

Anna: Thanks for explaining it so clearly. I can see how useful this can be in problem-solving.

Me: You're welcome, Anna. It's straightforward yet powerful, and when used correctly, it can make a significant difference in how effectively you solve problems. Just remember, it's all about systematically exploring causes, just like a detective piecing together clues to solve a mystery.

Anna: This all sounds very systematic. Can you summarise the key to effective problem-solving?

Me: Effective problem-solving requires a structured approach like DMAIC, but it also demands intuition, experience, and continuous improvement. Always validate problems and solutions, use consistent measurements, analyse deeply, and ensure controls are in place for predictability. It's about making the process as natural and intuitive as breathing, always aiming to eliminate issues at their root. By following this structured approach and focusing on key success factors at each phase, companies can effectively tackle problems and implement sustainable solutions, ensuring continuous improvement and success.

Homework:

With whom do you want to share your insights on Problem Solving?

Who will be your accountability buddy for handholding and implementing your insights?

How are you killing the problems you face and avoiding their recurrence?

One-on-one Dialogue

One-on-one dialogue is a crucial practice in business that provides a platform for open, heartfelt communication between managers and employees. These personal meetings foster trust, understanding, and transparency, allowing individuals to discuss their concerns, aspirations, and feedback in a safe and supportive environment. This approach helps in building stronger relationships, enhancing employee engagement, and addressing issues before they escalate. One-on-one dialogues also offer an opportunity for managers to provide personalised guidance, support professional development, and align individual goals with the broader objectives of the organisation. By investing in these meaningful conversations, businesses can cultivate a positive work culture and drive overall performance and satisfaction.

One-on-one dialogue creates bonds and builds trust in the CORE, SUSTAIN, and ADVANCE.

Introducing Beltrano, the plant manager of a medium-sized company in his late 40s, who faces extreme difficulty in delegating tasks and making time for himself. Beltrano is eager to explore how one-on-one dialogues can help him overcome these challenges and improve his management approach.

Beltrano: Hi, I've been struggling with delegating tasks and finding time for myself. I've heard that one-on-one dialogues might help. Can you share your thoughts on this? Why are these meetings so crucial?

Me: Great question, Beltrano. Weekly one-on-one dialogues are like the oil that keeps an engine running smoothly. They ensure that communication flows freely and that both the leader and the employee are aligned and working effectively together. It's a dedicated time for connection, feedback, and support.

Beltrano: But can't we just communicate through emails and team meetings?

Me: Emails and team meetings are essential, but they often lack the personal touch and depth of one-on-one conversations. Think of a one-on-one dialogue as a gardener tending to each plant individually. It allows for personalised care and attention, addressing specific needs and fostering growth in ways that group settings can't.

Beltrano: How does this personalised attention benefit the employee?

Me: It benefits the employee in several ways. First, it provides a safe space for them to share concerns, ideas, and feedback without the pressure of a group setting. It's like having a regular check-up with a doctor—issues can be identified and addressed early before they become bigger problems. It also builds trust and rapport, making the employee feel valued and heard.

Beltrano: And what about the leader? How do they benefit from these meetings?

Me: For the leader, one-on-one dialogues offer a clearer understanding of what's happening on the ground. It's like having a direct line to the frontlines, getting firsthand insights that might not come up in larger meetings. This helps in making informed decisions and providing targeted support. It also strengthens the relationship with the employee, fostering loyalty and engagement.

Beltrano: What topics should be covered in these one-on-one meetings?

Me: These meetings can cover a wide range of topics. Think of them as a toolbox with various tools for different tasks. They can include progress updates, goal setting, feedback, career development discussions, and personal well-being check-ins. It's important to balance addressing immediate tasks and long-term development, ensuring the employee feels supported in all aspects of their role.

Beltrano: How can leaders ensure these meetings are productive?

Me: Preparation is key. Both the leader and the employee should come prepared with topics to discuss. It's like preparing for a journey—you need to know your destination and the route to get there. Setting an agenda helps keep the meeting focused and ensures important points are covered. Regular follow-ups on action items from previous meetings also keep the momentum going. The most important though is that I have been using behavioural and analysis triangles before any such dialogue.

Beltrano: Yes. I've heard about the behaviour triangle for giving feedback. Could you explain it to me with some examples?

Me: Absolutely, Beltrano. The behaviour triangle is a tool for giving structured and effective feedback. Think of it as a map guiding a conversation about performance. There are three sides to this triangle: context, behaviour, and outcome. Let me illustrate it with a recent experience I had.

Beltrano: Sure, I'd love to hear about it.

Me: Yesterday, I was on a call with a director from a large multinational company. During the discussion, we talked about various tools and methods for improving business performance, including the importance of people over processes like PDCA, process mapping, or KPIs. The director highlighted that focusing on people is now the differentiator, assuming other processes are already in place. This set the stage for discussing the behaviour triangle.

Beltrano: That sounds interesting. So, how do you use the behaviour triangle in such scenarios?

Me: The behaviour triangle helps in observing and giving feedback. Imagine you need to give feedback to an employee about a missed deadline. First, you need to understand and convey the situation clearly. For example, "In our project meeting last week, we discussed the deadline for submitting the report."

Beltrano: Okay, that's setting the context. What comes next?

Me: Next is behaviour. You describe what you observed without judgement. "I noticed that the report wasn't submitted by the deadline, and there was no communication about the delay." It's crucial to stick to observable actions, like a detective reporting facts.

Beltrano: Got it. How do you wrap it up?

Me: The final part is the result. Explain the impact of the behaviour. "Because the report was late, we missed the opportunity to present our findings to the client, which could affect our relationship with them." This completes the triangle—situation, behaviour, and result.

Beltrano: That makes sense. But how do you use this feedback to actually help the employee improve?

Me: Great question! After outlining the behaviour triangle, I refer to three critical factors: goal, skill, and attitude. For instance, does the employee understand the goal? In our example, did they know why the report was crucial? It's like ensuring a driver knows the destination before starting the journey.

Beltrano: And what about skill and attitude?

Me: For skill, I ask if they have the ability to meet the goal. "Do you know how to gather and analyse the data for the report?" It's like checking if our driver has the necessary driving skills. For attitude, I explore their motivation. "Do you see the importance of meeting deadlines?" It's understanding if the driver wants to reach the destination and enjoys the journey.

Beltrano: So, it's about diagnosing the root cause behind the performance issue?

Me: Exactly. By understanding the goal, skill, and attitude, we can provide targeted support. If the goal isn't clear, I'll clarify it. If the skill is lacking, I'll provide training. If the attitude needs adjustment, I'll explore underlying motivations. It's like fine-tuning a car to ensure a smooth ride.

Beltrano: That's insightful. Can you give an example of a positive outcome using this method?

Me: Sure. Let's say an employee consistently exceeds expectations. Using the behaviour triangle, I would acknowledge the situation: "In our last three projects, you completed tasks ahead of schedule." Highlight the behaviour: "You proactively communicated with team members and managed your time effectively." And explain the result: "This helped us meet our project goals early, earning praise from the client." Then, I'd reinforce the positive goal, skill, and attitude to encourage continued success.

Beltrano: This seems like a comprehensive approach. Does it take a lot of time to implement?

Me: Initially, it might take some time to get used to the method, but once you and your team are familiar with it, the behaviour triangle becomes a natural part of your feedback process. It's like learning to ride a bike—challenging at first but effortless once you've got the hang of it. And the benefits, like improved performance and stronger relationships, are well worth the investment.

Beltrano: Now that I understand how to give meaningful feedback, can you give an example of a successful one-on-one dialogue?

Me: Sure! Imagine an employee struggling with a project. In a one-on-one, the leader can delve into the specifics, offering guidance and resources to overcome obstacles. They can also provide constructive feedback and recognise the employee's efforts. This personalised support can boost the employee's confidence and motivation, much like a coach helping an athlete refine their technique and achieve their best performance.

Beltrano: What if an employee doesn't feel comfortable sharing openly in these meetings?

Me: Building trust takes time. It's important for the leader to create a safe and non-judgemental environment. It's like planting seeds in a garden—you need patience and consistent care for them to grow. Encouraging open dialogue, showing empathy, and being genuinely interested in the employee's well-being can help them open up over time.

Beltrano: How do these one-on-one dialogues fit into the bigger picture of team management?

Me: One-on-one dialogues complement other team management practices by ensuring individual attention. It's like tuning individual instruments in an orchestra to create a harmonious performance. When each team member feels supported and aligned with the team's goals, overall performance improves, leading to greater success for the entire organisation.

Beltrano: This all makes sense. What are some success factors for one-on-one dialogues?

Me: There are a few key success factors to keep in mind. First, the baseline for the dialogue should be the assigned tasks, their current status, the routines needed from the role, their actual doing, and the notes from the earlier one-on-one dialogue. This is like setting up a foundation before building a house.

Beltrano: How do you start the dialogue effectively?

Me: Begin by listening to the employee's perspective on their tasks and any challenges they're facing. It's important to hear them out fully before jumping in with recommendations. Think of it as a doctor listening to a patient's symptoms before diagnosing and prescribing treatment.

Beltrano: What happens after listening to the employee?

Me: After listening, provide your recommendations to help them overcome their challenges. This ensures the employee feels heard and supported. It's like a coach providing feedback after watching an athlete's performance, offering specific advice to improve.

Beltrano: Is there anything else that should be included in these meetings?

Me: Yes, picking a random topic for mutual discussion can be very beneficial. It's like exploring uncharted territory together, allowing for mutual learning and fostering a deeper connection. This can be about industry trends, personal development topics, or any subject of interest.

Beltrano: How do you wrap up the meeting?

Me: Conclude the session by noting down the outcomes and any action items. This helps in keeping track of progress and ensures accountability. It's like summarising the main points of a journey before setting off on the next leg, making sure everyone knows their next steps.

Beltrano: This sounds very comprehensive. Any final thoughts?

Me: Consistency is key. Make these meetings a regular part of your routine, not just an occasional check-in. It's like maintaining a healthy diet—you need regular, balanced meals to stay healthy, not just a feast once in a while. Regular one-on-one dialogues build a strong foundation for ongoing communication, trust, and development, leading to a more engaged and productive team. Weekly one-on-one dialogues between a leader and their employee are invaluable for fostering open communication, providing personalised support, and building a strong, trusting relationship that benefits both the individual and the organisation.

Homework:

With whom do you want to share your insights on One-on-one Dialogue?

Who will be your accountability buddy for handholding and implementing your insights?

How are you serving your colleagues by coaching and developing them to supersede you?

Leveraging Technology

Leveraging technology is crucial for modern businesses to enhance efficiency, productivity, and innovation by making work easier and enabling smart working. The right technology platforms can streamline processes, automate repetitive tasks, and provide real-time data insights, allowing employees to focus on more strategic and creative aspects of their roles. Effective use of technology improves communication and collaboration, breaks down silos, and fosters a more agile and responsive organisational culture. However, it is essential to choose and implement technology thoughtfully to ensure it truly addresses the needs of the business and integrates seamlessly into existing workflows. When done correctly, leveraging technology can transform the way a business operates, leading to significant improvements in performance and competitiveness.

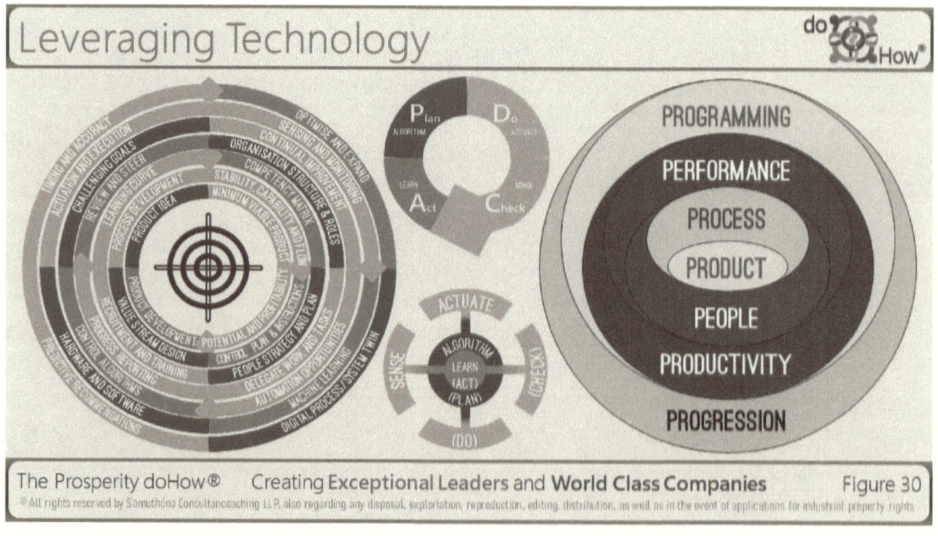

The Prosperity doHow® Creating Exceptional Leaders and World Class Companies Figure 30

Leveraging technology makes our life easier with time to focus on the important, instead of spending time on preparation and follow-up in the CORE, SUSTAIN, and ADVANCE.

Introducing Vasily, the CTO of a large company in his late 40s, who is intrigued by the fact that various technology platforms have not made life easier. Vasily is interested in discussing how to effectively leverage technology to truly enhance work processes and productivity.

Vasily: Hi, I'm intrigued by the fact that despite having various technology platforms, we haven't seen significant improvements in making work easier. I've been hearing a lot about digitisation and digitalisation lately. Are they the same thing?

Me: Great question, Vasily! Though they sound similar, digitisation and digitalisation are quite different, much like the difference between taking a photo of a paper document and creating an interactive app for managing documents. Let's dive into it.

Vasily: I'm curious, can you explain digitisation first?

Me: Absolutely! Digitisation is the process of converting analogue information into digital format. Think of it as taking a physical book and scanning each page to create a PDF. The information remains the same, but now it's in a digital form that can be easily stored, accessed, and shared.

Vasily: So, it's like turning old records into MP3 files?

Me: Exactly! Digitisation is about creating a digital version of something physical. It's the first step in the journey towards more advanced digital processes, making information more accessible and easier to manipulate.

Vasily: And how about digitalisation? How is it different?

Me: Digitalisation, on the other hand, is about using digital technology to transform business operations and processes. It's like taking that scanned book and creating an e-learning platform where students can interact with the content, take quizzes, and track their progress. It's not just about converting information but also enhancing and transforming how we use it.

Vasily: So, digitalisation is more about changing the way we work with information?

Me: Precisely. Digitalisation leverages technology to improve efficiency, enhance customer experiences, and create new value. For example, a digitised document can be stored and retrieved easily, but a digitalised document management system can automate workflows, enable remote collaboration, and provide analytics to improve decision-making.

Vasily: Can you give an example of digitalisation in action?

Me: Sure! Imagine a traditional retail store digitises its inventory by using barcodes and a digital database. That's digitisation. When the store uses this digital inventory to implement an online shopping platform, integrates it with supply chain management, and uses data analytics to predict trends and manage stock levels, that's digitalisation. It transforms the business model and operations entirely.

Vasily: So, in essence, digitisation is about converting, and digitalisation is about transforming?

Me: Exactly, Vasily. Digitisation is the foundation—it's essential for getting started on the digital journey. Digitalisation builds on that foundation to create new opportunities, streamline processes, and improve overall business performance. It's like building a house on a solid base and then turning it into a smart home. Leveraging technology is digitalisation.

Vasily: I've heard the term "leveraging technology" quite a bit. Can you explain what it really means and how it can benefit a business?

Me: Sure, Vasily! Leveraging technology is essentially about using both hardware and software to manage repetitive tasks efficiently within an environment. It's like having a highly skilled assistant who takes care of routine tasks so you can focus on more strategic activities. This approach is structured around the Plan-Do-Check-Act (PDCA) cycle, which ensures continuous improvement and adaptability.

Vasily: How does the PDCA cycle fit into leveraging technology?

Me: The PDCA cycle is integral to leveraging technology. It's a systematic approach to problem-solving and process improvement. Think of it like a chef perfecting a recipe:

Plan (Algorithm): This is where we design the strategy. It's like drafting a detailed recipe. For instance, in a business context, we might outline the steps for automating a customer service process.

Do (Actuate): Here, we execute the plan. It's similar to cooking according to the recipe. We implement the automation using the chosen technology.

Check (Sense): This step involves monitoring and evaluating the results. Imagine the chef tasting the dish to ensure it's perfect. In business, we analyse the performance of the automated process, gathering feedback and metrics.

Act (Learn): Based on the feedback, we make necessary adjustments. The chef might tweak the seasoning to enhance the dish. In business, we refine the process to improve efficiency and outcomes.

Vasily: Can you break down this PDCA cycle for me?

Me: Certainly! The PDCA cycle is a continuous loop of planning, executing, checking, and acting to ensure ongoing improvement. It's like a chef constantly tasting and adjusting a dish to achieve the perfect flavour.

Vasily: How does this apply to different cycles like product, process, and people?

Me: Let's dive into each one.

Vasily: What's the first step in the product cycle?

Me: The first step is the Plan phase. This stage involves ideation workshops and market trend analysis to generate product ideas. It's like planting seeds in a fertile garden, ensuring a variety of plants can grow.

Vasily: What happens after the planning?

Me: Next, we move to the Do phase. Here, we implement the plan by prototyping and testing these ideas. It's akin to nurturing the seedlings with water and sunlight. Technologies like CAD/CAM and 3D printing play a crucial role in this phase.

Vasily: How do we know if our prototypes are good?

Me: That's where the Check phase comes in. After developing prototypes, we gather feedback from focus groups and analyse the product's potential and profitability, much like a gardener checking the health and growth of the plants.

Vasily: And the final step?

Me: Finally, we Act by refining the product based on the feedback and preparing for market launch. This is similar to pruning and shaping the plants for the best yield.

Vasily: How about the process cycle? What's the starting point?

Me: We start with the Plan phase, which involves designing value streams and making critical process decisions, such as whether to make or buy certain components. It's like mapping out the most efficient route for a road trip.

Vasily: What do we do after planning?

Me: The Do phase follows, where we develop the process, including tooling and material handling. This is similar to preparing the vehicle and ensuring it's in top condition for the journey.

Vasily: How do we ensure the process is working well?

Me: In the Check phase, we evaluate the process's stability and capability, much like checking the car's performance and making sure it's running smoothly.

Vasily: And finally?

Me: The Act phase involves implementing control strategies and optimising the process, akin to adjusting the route based on real-time traffic updates to ensure the smoothest travel.

Vasily: What about the people cycle?

Me: We begin with the Plan phase, creating a people strategy, including hiring plans and job descriptions. It's like assembling a team for a sports league, ensuring each member's role is well-defined.

Vasily: What's the next step?

Me: The Do phase involves recruiting and training employees, similar to conducting team practices and drills to build skills and teamwork.

Vasily: How do we track their performance?

Me: In the Check phase, we monitor performance and training effectiveness, much like a coach analysing game footage to identify areas for improvement.

Vasily: And finally?

Me: The Act phase involves adjusting training programs and roles based on feedback, ensuring continuous improvement, like modifying practice routines to enhance team performance.

Vasily: What's the focus of the performance cycle?

Me: The Plan phase here involves setting the vision, mission, and strategic goals, much like a captain plotting the course for a voyage.

Vasily: And then?

Me: In the Do phase, we delegate tasks and responsibilities, similar to assigning roles to the crew and ensuring everyone knows their duties.

Vasily: How do we ensure we're on the right track?

Me: The Check phase involves monitoring performance through dashboards and reports, akin to checking the ship's instruments and logs to ensure it's on course.

Vasily: And the last step?

Me: The Act phase involves reviewing and steering the organisation based on performance data, adjusting the course as needed to reach the destination.

Vasily: How do we enhance productivity?

Me: We start with the Plan phase, setting challenging goals and benchmarking against best practices, like aiming to break a sports record.

Vasily: What's next?

Me: The Do phase involves implementing continuous improvement initiatives and automating repetitive tasks, similar to an athlete practising and refining their techniques.

Vasily: How do we measure productivity?

Me: In the Check phase, we measure productivity through various metrics, much like tracking an athlete's performance stats.

Vasily: And finally?

Me: The Act phase involves refining our processes and strategies to optimise productivity, akin to a coach making strategic adjustments based on performance data.

Vasily: How about the programming cycle?

Me: The Plan phase involves designing and planning the integration of hardware and software, much like an architect designing a smart home with integrated systems.

Vasily: And then?

Me: In the Do phase, we execute the plan by deploying actuators, sensors, and software, similar to installing and configuring the smart home systems.

Vasily: How do we ensure everything works?

Me: The Check phase involves monitoring the systems to ensure they function correctly, like checking the smart home's performance through a central dashboard.

Vasily: And the final step?

Me: The Act phase involves adjusting and optimising the systems based on monitoring, akin to updating and fine-tuning the smart home settings.

Vasily: Lastly, what about the progression cycle?

Me: The Plan phase involves simulating processes and validating them through experiments, like a scientist designing and testing hypotheses in a lab.

Vasily: What's the next step?

Me: The Do phase involves implementing recommendations and monitoring outcomes, similar to conducting experiments and observing results.

Vasily: How do we ensure accuracy?

Me: In the Check phase, we track the accuracy and timeliness of our recommendations, like analysing lab results for consistency and reliability.

Vasily: And finally?

Me: The Act phase involves learning from the outcomes to refine our models and strategies, akin to a scientist publishing findings and iterating on future research.

In essence, each cycle follows the PDCA approach to ensure continuous improvement, much like a conductor ensuring all musicians are in harmony for a flawless performance.

Vasily: Can you give an example of how this works in practice?

Me: Absolutely. Take the example of a customer service department. Traditionally, handling customer inquiries involves a lot of repetitive tasks. By leveraging technology, we can use chatbots to handle common queries, freeing up human agents for more complex issues.

First, we Plan by identifying the most common questions customers ask. Then, we Do by programming a chatbot to respond to these questions. We Check by monitoring how well the chatbot handles inquiries and gathering customer feedback. Finally, we Act by refining the chatbot's responses based on the feedback to ensure it provides accurate and helpful answers.

Vasily: That sounds efficient. What are the broader benefits of leveraging technology in this way?

Me: The benefits are substantial. By automating repetitive tasks, businesses can improve efficiency, reduce errors, and save time. This allows employees to focus on higher-value activities, such as innovation and customer engagement. It's like upgrading from manual tools to advanced machinery in a factory – the output increases, the quality improves, and the workers can focus on more skilled tasks.

With whom do you want to share your insights on Leveraging Technology?

Who will be your accountability buddy for handholding and implementing your insights?

How are you identifying the automation opportunities and leveraging technology to make your work and life easier?

doHow® Implementation Tips

1. CORE: Seek a coach, either internal or an external doHow® Coach, for handholding to implement CORE. This is the foundation necessary to accelerate the doHow® Implementation.

2. SUSTAIN: Review the maturity of each of the elements of SUSTAIN along with the coach to identify the strengths and weaknesses for the right focus during the implementation of doHow®.

3. ADVANCE: Prepare an ADVANCE roadmap to implement doHow® along with the coach with macro timelines, however extending to a maximum of six months.

4. Sales and Operations: Implement quick fixes for generating cash, so that the implementation of doHow® can be done without any major interruptions in the rhythm chakra. In case even the quick fixes take time, have patience, implement them before trying to ADVANCE.

5. Leading versus Managing: Get the coach to facilitate a session for debating on leading and managing for increasing the awareness of both and for everyone to identify their top focus area to balance their leadership and management behaviour for accelerating the implementation of doHow®.

6. Mastering Time Management: Get everyone to analyse their activities for creating sufficient time to focus on implementing doHow®, using the coach if needed.

7. Mindset and Culture: Get the coach to facilitate a session for debating on mindset and culture for increasing the awareness of both and for everyone to develop patience and resilience in coping with their own behaviour and that of others during the implementation of doHow®.

8. Stakeholder Analysis: Get the key players to analyse/ review their stakeholders, both personal and professional, before getting the coach to facilitate group work to arrive at the common understanding on the expectations of the professional stakeholders, as a starting point to implement doHow®.

9. Prosperity Chakras: Get the key players to assess the maturity of the business chakras, before getting the coach to facilitate group work to arrive at the common understanding on expectations of the current reality, as another starting point to implement doHow®.

10. Progressive Maturity Scale: Get the coach to facilitate a session for debating on the progressive maturity scale for developing the capability to uniformly assess the maturity during the implementation of doHow®.

11. 360° Goal Setting: Get the coach to facilitate a session for discussing on the various goal domains, for choosing/ reviewing top three focus areas with aspirational goals for the implementation of doHow®.

12. Inspirational Persuasion: Get the coach to facilitate a session for developing broad strategies using contextual hints based on the stakeholder expectations and the current reality, followed by defining/reviewing the top-level key performance indicators and their owners.

13. Key Performance Indicators: Get the KPI owners to cascade the KPIs and assign/review the lower level KPI owners, with the support of the coach as and when needed, covering all the aspects of the business.

14. Rolling Planning: Get the KPI owners to define/review the rolling plans based on the top-level plans at the defined clockspeeds (Yearly, Quarterly, Monthly, Weekly, Daily) for the previous time zone (Actual), current time zone (Estimate), next time zone (Plan), time zone after next (Forecast) and the time three time zones from the current one (Target), by seeking the help of the coach if needed.

15. Job Role Description: Get the KPI owners to define/review the descriptions of all the roles necessary for meeting the respective KPI and in case of common roles, ensure that the requirements of all the KPI owners is incorporated in such roles, by using the help of the coach if needed, for clarifying the expectations for each role.

16. Creating and Implementing Standards: Get the KPI owners to define/review the standards necessary for ensuring consistent performance and delivery by all the defined roles, by using the help of the coach if needed, to enable seamless delegation and monitoring/control of the performance.

17. Business Process Excellence: Get the KPI owners to describe the process steps necessary to fulfil the KPIs along with defining the Responsible, Approver, Collaborator, Supporter and Information Recipient, so that each of them can then define/review the key success factors and key performance metrics, especially the drivers metrics, for their roles, by using the help of the coach if needed, to enable a fresher to start performing and delivering using the process. If needed revisit the Job Role Descriptions and the cascaded KPIs, so that there is 100% match and harmony.

18. Project for Tasks: Get the KPI owners to create templates for projects along with full-kit checklists for taking over and handing over tasks, so that the tasks seamlessly transition through the project, by using the help of the coach if needed,

to enable a fresher to start performing and delivering using these templates.

19. Continuous Manufacturing Flow: Get the KPI owners to map and describe/review the value stream for seamless flow, ideally with Ø waste, for consistently delivering the value to the customers, by using the help of the coach if needed. If needed revisit the Job Role Descriptions, the cascaded KPIs, the Process Descriptions and Project Templates so that there is 100% match and harmony.

20. Execution Planning: Get the KPI owners to define/review routines based on described processes and one-time actions based on project templates for achieving the plan time zone of the rolling plan, however aiming for at least 20% better than the plan for accommodating unforeseen surprises along the way, by using the help of the coach if needed, for fulfilling the plan against all odds.

21. Regular Reporting: Get the entire organisation to report the progress of their activities, preferably in a technology platform, and create dashboards for everyone authorised in the organisation to know the status, by using the help of the coach if needed, at a clockspeed faster than the one used for the execution planning.

22. Regular Steering: Define/review the steering panels, and if needed update the process descriptions, to discuss the progress reports, under the guidance of the coach, for efficient and effective reviews.

23. Problem Solving: Choose the top problems identified during the regular steering based on the pareto principle, form a cross-functional team and solve the problem, with the support of the coach if needed, to kill the problem and avoid recurrence.

24. One-on-one Dialogue: Get every leader/manager to conduct one-on-one dialogues with his/her team members using the

reported performance as evidence, if needed, with the coach as an observer, to encourage and demand the team member to develop further and perform better.

25. Leveraging Technology: Once the doHow® practices are implemented and they have stabilised, start identifying the automation opportunities during the regular steering reviews, define/review the control cycle and automate using technology for making life easier to every user, by using the help of the coach if needed, to use the technology as an enabler and not as a deterrent to the intrinsically capable and intelligent people.

The implementation of doHow® can also be done by writing to marketing@samuthana.com or visiting https://app.businessdohow.com/ and using the doHow® Performance Excellence Platform (PEP) application.

Last but not the least, it is important to mention that doHow® is a fully integrated closed-loop system for global optimum, that may seem complex, but once implemented, any organisation can become a learning organisation within about six months. At the same time, it is important to remember that implementing individual elements of doHow®, which may seem simpler, will make the organisation sluggish due to the separate functioning of each of the elements for a local optimum.

A Success Story

Reflecting on a chaotic day with lots of crises to manage and almost nothing completed from the To-Do list, Arjun remembers hearing about The Prosperity doHow® for performance excellence, a Socratic Learning Methodology. He discovers Drona as a doHow® Coach while searching on LinkedIn and sends a connection request with a short message. Drona, just before sleeping, checks LinkedIn, accepts the connection request, and suggests discussing the next day anytime in the afternoon.

Arjun is an ambitious budding graduate with a dream of leaving behind a legacy. He thinks a lot to find answers and is very much self-motivated. However, he is trying hard to find a better way of working for a better work/life balance. Drona is a freelance trainer and consultant with more than twenty-five years of corporate experience in various leadership roles. He got excited about The Prosperity doHow® and has become a doHow® Coach. He loves flexible working while helping people and companies excel.

Arjun and Drona introduce themselves and discuss the first step in the doHow® Performance Excellence Platform (https://app.businessdohow.com/), focusing on the time management and stakeholder assessment modules, which can be done without any licence. Arjun gets excited with the guided hints in the time management module after signing up and thanks Drona for the help.

Arjun is excited about the insights he derived from the time management module and shares them with Heinrich at the lunch table. Having completed his masters in various business planning programs, Heinrich has implemented rolling planning in the Contract Manufacturing Company to provide consistency for operations while being agile for catering to fluctuating market demands. The German is very impressed with the focus on basics in the doHow® Performance Excellence Platform and wants to know more. Arjun recommends the Stakeholder Assessment module to Heinrich.

doHow® Performance Excellence Platform

Individual and Company/Team Goal Setting	Business Chakras for Rapid Reality Assessment	Stakeholder Mapping	Market Analysis for Identifying the Blue Ocean Strategy	Market Canvas for Identifying the Key Differentiators	Sales Pitch Development
Common Understanding of Current Reality	Gamification for Contextual Inspirational Persuasion	Guided Policy/Target Deployment	Daily, Weekly, Monthly, Quarterly Rolling Planning	Target/Occupier Role Competencies Mapping	Guided Problem Solving
Guided Business Process Mapping	Guided Value Stream Mapping			Guided Execution Planning	Onetime Tasks and Recurring Activities Management
Fullkit Planning and Monitoring	Structured After Action Review	dohow.samuthana.com		Performance Ranking Progress Scoreboard	Continual Improvement Monitoring
Regular Performance Reporting	Structured Performance Review			Guided 1-on-1 Dialogue	Audit Planning, Execution and Closure Monitoring
Workflow Automation with Checklist/Photo	360° Leadership Feedback and Assessment	doHow® Time Management Optimiser	doHow® Behaviour Analysis	doHow® Transformation Program	doHow® Transformation Modules
doHow® Socratic Module Elements	doHow® Homework Module Elements	doHow® User Management	doHow® Payment Workflow	Structured Mentoring, Training, Coaching Workflow	Structured Knowledge Monetisation

The Prosperity doHow®   Creating Exceptional Leaders and World Class Companies   Figure 31

Heinrich signs up to check out the stakeholder assessment but first wants to understand the entire doHow® Performance Excellence Platform, as he is not satisfied with the overall experience of the stakeholders of the Contract Manufacturing Company despite his painstaking efforts in preparing a realistic rolling plan. He downloads the user manual using the link provided in the app after logging in. Being very meticulous in his approach, he decides to read the entire user manual before checking out either the time management or stakeholder assessment modules. Heinrich is even more impressed with just the basics being addressed in the doHow® Performance Excellence Platform and starts exploring the time management module.

He resonates with the time management strategies suggested and is excited to explore the stakeholder assessment. The suggested success strategies further inspire him, and he is able to relate very well as he enters all his stakeholders, people either benefiting from his contribution or those people necessary to enhance his contribution. A rating of the success strategy execution impresses him the most, since this drives deep reflection and thereby naturally creates self-drive to excel. He is now convinced that the doHow® Performance Excellence Platform, based on a Socratic Learning Methodology, can be of great help in improving the effectiveness of the Contract Manufacturing Company while improving efficiency within and decides to speak about using this platform to Julio, a seasoned, ambitious operations leader and Heinrich's boss, in his mid-40s who has been with the Contract Manufacturing Company since its inception and has worked in all the functions before heading operations and understands the key drivers for performance excellence.

Heinrich arrives ahead of the scheduled meeting at Julio's office, a neatly maintained space with a display of the latest updated performance dashboards. Julio asks Heinrich to take a seat at the meeting table as he is busy with an email reply. Julio moves to the meeting table, attentively listens to what Heinrich has to say, agrees to explore the doHow® Socratic Learning Methodology after some clarification questions, and suggests organising a meeting with the doHow® Coach along with the key players for understanding the doHow® Performance Excellence Platform, based on a Socratic Learning Methodology.

Heinrich leaves satisfied as he calls Arjun from his mobile, requesting him to introduce him to the doHow® Coach. Arjun is excited with the news and offers to coordinate the meeting with the doHow® Coach.

Arjun is excited to meet Drona, the doHow® Coach, who arrives ten minutes early and sets up his computer for any eventual presentation that may be needed. After the initial pleasantries, they settle down, sipping coffee as they wait for the others to join.

Heinrich walks in and introduces himself, complimenting Drona on the very interesting and inspiring work done. Mohammed, the sales key account manager, walks in next. A seasoned B2B sales executive, Mohammed has acquired exceptional prospecting skills the hard way and is instrumental in realising the growth ambitions of the Contract Manufacturing Company. He believes acquiring clients and orders is easy, but retaining them is a challenge due to the shabby performance of operations, which always have a reason for missing timelines. He walks in with a lot of apprehension, fearing this might be another brainwashing session.

Naomi, the supply chain manager, enters next with her supply chain experience from the extremely complex eCommerce business, which makes her believe that managing the team for sourcing just a few components in the Contract Manufacturing Company is a cakewalk. She still finds it difficult to understand why her team members are struggling so much and working almost 24x7. Geetha, the HR executive, walks in together with Naomi, discussing the outcome of an interview they had for a buyer role. After a brief internship in a software company, Geetha recently joined the Contract Manufacturing Company HR team and is really surprised at the almost cold people practices, with slow progression and rare rewards and recognition compared to the software industry. She is still trying to understand the people drivers in an environment where there is hardly any tracking.

Finally, Julio walks in with Tadashi, the quality manager, introducing him as the one driving all improvements in the Contract Manufacturing Company. Coming from a TQM background, Tadashi has been trying hard to implement the traditional PDCA cycle in all the activities of the Contract Manufacturing Company, with little success since the day-to-day work is rather chaotic with a lot of surprises, making the quality department face the customer for missing out on improvement commitments made.

With everyone present, Julio briefly introduces the Contract Manufacturing Company and explains their challenges along with his analysis of the cause and effect. He then asks others to add their comments before Drona explains the doHow® Value Proposition. Drona listens to each of their explanations of the challenges and their understanding of the cause and effect.

It is now clear to Drona that each of them is doing their best from their own perspective, while the challenges still persist.

Drona chooses to just talk with no presentation, as he explains The Prosperity doHow® and the doHow® Performance Excellence Platform, based on a Socratic Learning Methodology, with some case studies. He introduces the three core ideas: CORE, SUSTAIN, and ADVANCE. The Contract Manufacturing Team resonates with whatever Drona explains, already starts thinking, and asks for a proposal to be made for taking the next steps. Almost unanimously, Arjun gets nominated as the single point of contact. Drona leaves inspired by the challenges.

Drona is excited with the outcome of the meeting at the Contract Manufacturing Company and meticulously prepares and sends the proposal to Arjun for perusal. Arjun promptly processes the proposal from Drona and, after getting the budgetary approvals, passes it on to Naomi to discuss with Drona and finalise the PO for starting the assignment.

Drona is surprised to receive a call from Naomi within three days of sending the proposal, based on ADVANCE. He answers her call with surprise and excitement as they speak on how a comparable offer can be gathered for the L1 principle of the Contract Manufacturing Company to be met. Drona explains that doHow® being an innovation, there is nothing comparable in the market. One-on-one executive coaching could be the closest since doHow® primarily gets people reflecting and thinking to discover their own success strategies after enabling the understanding of the context from different perspectives. Drona explains that the per person doHow® Performance Execution Platform pricing is extremely competitive in comparison with executive coaching and, of course, much higher than training, which doesn't necessarily drive results. Naomi understands the logic and expresses her displeasure with the way the negotiation discussion is going. After discussing multiple options, they conclude on a 2% discount, discuss a date for the kick-off, and conclude the discussion.

Naomi informs Arjun to speak to Drona and organise the kick-off meeting. Arjun gets in touch with Drona to discuss the modus operandi. Drona suggests planning fortnightly three-hour sessions for six months, either face-to-face or virtual depending on the agenda, so that the normally two-hour session, even if it extends, can be completed within three hours. They agree upon alternating Thursdays from 10:00 to 13:00 as the best option. Drona further mentions that the kick-off may be a virtual one since the agenda mainly involves explaining the preparation for the Stakeholder workshop.

Drona gets Arjun on a Teams call and shares his desktop screen as he creates Arjun as a doHow® Performance Excellence Platform user in the Contract Manufacturing Company. Arjun follows attentively and keeps asking questions to understand the flow.

Then Drona purchases a client licence with Arjun as the Admin for twenty-five users. He then creates a hierarchy for Arjun as the Admin and requests him to create all the others as doHow® Performance Excellence Platform users and then create their reporting hierarchies.

Arjun creates all the users and their hierarchy relationships and gets Drona on a Teams call to show what he had done and to get his executive defined as Julio. Now they are all set for the virtual kick-off.

Drona reminds Arjun to request the participants to log in to the kick-off Teams call from their respective workplaces, so that they can check out and experience the doHow® Performance Excellence Platform, which they will be using during the entire program.

On Thursday, February 10, 2022, the entire team logs in to Teams five minutes ahead of 10:00 from their respective workplaces and waits for Drona to join. Drona joins two minutes ahead of 10:00 so that they could start on time.

Drona acknowledges the punctuality and, after briefly exchanging greetings for the day, shares his screen and checks if everyone is able to see and hear him.

Everyone either logs in to the doHow® Performance Excellence Platform or signs up. Drona logs in to the doHow® Performance Excellence Platform and first explains how to download the user manual, before taking them through the user manual for each of them to go through as homework and familiarise themselves with the doHow® Performance Excellence Platform.

He then explains the Stakeholder module and creates two breakout rooms for them to just try out the module, discuss, and return with questions. After the short breakout session, Naomi wants to know which stakeholders to assess.

Drona mentions that they should assess all the stakeholders who are necessary for each of them to feel successful in their personal and professional lives. He also mentions that during the next face-to-face Stakeholder Expectations workshop only the professional stakeholders will be discussed.

Heinrich wants to know if they can already initiate a task or routine. Drona says that they surely can, so that they can start reporting with immediate effect.

Julio says he is already seeing the benefits of using doHow®.

Tadashi says he is relieved since they are starting with the Voice of the Customer.

Geetha and Mohammed say that they are excited with the homework.

Drona concludes the doHow® session five minutes ahead of 12:00 with two assignments till the next session, which he enters in the doHow® session report:

1. Familiarise with the user manual.

2. Complete Stakeholder Assessment.

Everyone at Contract Manufacturing Company discusses the thoughts provoked by the doHow® session during lunch and gets busy with their daily routine. Everyone updates their already long To-Do list with another item to read the doHow® manual. Drona, as a standard practice, sends out an encouragement email after one week and reminds everyone to complete the Stakeholder Assessment. Heinrich, who has by this time completed his Stakeholder Assessment, updating every time he remembered a new important stakeholder, replies to Drona's email to all, something he rarely does, explaining his experiences with the Stakeholder Assessment and how this has already helped him in making his work/life more purposeful – a very strong statement indeed.

Arjun hurriedly completes his Stakeholder Assessment and replies to Heinrich's email (to all) mentioning his achievement. He doesn't want to be left behind and be labelled as the odd man out since he is ambitious and wants to be in everyone's good books.

Julio thinks of delegating his Stakeholder Assessment and, after thorough consideration, decides to do it himself. Halfway through, he gets his Eureka moment while working on the Stakeholder Assessment at home. He realises how he hasn't been satisfying and delighting his reportees, an important stakeholder segment, by staying far from them.

Mohammed sees Heinrich's email and wonders why he is so excited about doing something so basic. He believes that being in sales, he has learnt the hard way to understand the expectations of people quickly as he gets into a conversation and gauges them quite accurately. He sets off with the Stakeholder Assessment and feels inspired to confirm to himself that he has been consistently practising the suggested strategies. He now feels closely connected to the doHow® Performance Excellence Platform and is comforted by the benefits the Contract Manufacturing Company will derive from it.

Naomi and Geetha decide to do the Stakeholder Assessment together. Both of them log in to the doHow® Performance Excellence Platform and start by entering their first stakeholder and speaking out to each other as they progress with the assessment of interest and influence. They become silent as they choose their level of consistency in executing the strategy. They then add on a couple of their other stakeholders and start discussing the drivers which lead them to not executing the strategies they agree are the most appropriate ones. As they conclude the Stakeholder Assessment, they express their expectations from the doHow® Performance Excellence Platform in helping them with better execution so that their effectiveness improves.

Tadashi, being very prompt in his work, completes his Stakeholder Assessment when Heinrich's email arrives. He is pleased that others are equally inspired by the doHow® Performance Excellence Platform. He is eager to discuss all the assessments and evolve a common understanding, especially of the voice of the customer, the primary driver of TQM.

Drona checks out the Stakeholder Assessments done on the evening of Wednesday, February 13, 2022, and is pleased that everyone has completed them as discussed. He also sees that most of them have initiated tasks and routines too. He takes a listing of all the professional stakeholders entered as a handout for the face-to-face doHow® session the next day.

Drona arrives at Contract Manufacturing Company thirty minutes ahead of schedule on Thursday, February 14, 2022, and gets Arjun to print two sets of the Stakeholder listing for the workshop. Once everyone is present, Julio starts with a brief greeting, and Drona takes over. Drona thanks and compliments everyone for completing the Stakeholder Assessment and splits them into two teams.

Julio, Geetha, and Tadashi form one team, and Arjun, Heinrich, Mohammed, and Naomi form the other. He hands over the handout to them and then asks them to discuss and agree upon the professional stakeholders of the Contract Manufacturing Company in each of the seven categories and their expectations.

Drona connects his laptop to the projector and starts entering the expectations of each of the Stakeholder groups, after a brief discussion, in the doHow® session report and keeps checking if they want any additional task or routine planned for any of these. This interactive discussion combined with the discussions between the groups takes about two hours. Drona keeps updating the doHow® session notes as well as the Expectations, Challenges, and Strategies, and keeps saving as a draft to avoid losing any data in case of a bug. Everyone is exhausted by the end of this important team exercise.

Drona explains the next steps of establishing a common understanding after saving the doHow® session report as a draft. Drona now gets everyone to stretch out a bit for the next small step of launching the Prosperity Chakra Assessment.

After a short discussion, Drona enters the market need fulfilled by the Contract Manufacturing Company for launching the Business Assessment. He explains how the anonymous Business Assessment needs to be done as homework until the next session. They conclude the meeting and head for lunch.

Drona, as usual, sends out a reminder to Arjun after checking the progress made on the assessment one week later. Arjun sees

Drona's email and calls him back to assure him that he is on top of the assessments, and it will be done ahead of the next face-to-face session.

On the night of Wednesday, March 9, 2022, Drona creates a PDF of the results of the business assessments and thinks through the face-to-face session for the next day.

On Thursday, March 10, 2022, Drona arrives thirty minutes ahead of schedule to get the printouts of the business assessment results for the group discussion. After everyone arrives on time for the doHow® session, Drona quickly divides them into two teams.

The teams then get busy going through the individual anonymous business assessments as they now need to seek the evidence and validate it before making their choices. Mohammed and Heinrich agree to enter their respective team choices in the APP as they leave the conference hall to seek the evidence in the Gemba (Workplace). This Teamwork is even more inspiring and enlightening to all as they together look at their current reality and many a times find it strange why many obviously simple jobs have become so complex with the common sense becoming so uncommon.

After about ninety minutes, everyone return to the conference hall after submitting their team assessments.

Drona now opens the same business assessment module and enters the consensus validation code to begin the assessment. But for three topics which lead to a healthy discussion between the teams before reaching a consensus, the other choices are identical between the teams. This assessment takes about one hour, extending the doHow® session beyond two hours to the buffer zone. Drona is calm and knows he can conclude within the planned three hours. He opens the doHow® session report again and makes note of the top challenges as per the common understanding of the reality under Expectations, Challenges and

Strategies and makes note of the Stakeholder Expectations for everyone to start identifying the strategies, already being executed and the new ones for meeting the Stakeholder Expectations. He submits the doHow® sessions report and concludes five minutes ahead of 13:00 as everyone head out for lunch.

That day in the afternoon, during their weekly operations review, Julio already speaks of some tweaks in their planning to fulfil their customer expectations better. Heinrich agrees to the suggestions almost spontaneously, against the normal practice of asking for a breather to evaluate the pros and cons. Tadashi is surprised at the way the doHow® Performance Excellence Platform has brought customer orientation. Mohammed is excited at not answering customer concerns on missed deliveries. Naomi cautions that this dream state may take some time. Geetha shares her experiences with the HR team, as she mentions the way doHow® has inspired everyone. Arjun is really happy and sees his brand equity growing from him introducing doHow® to the Contract Manufacturing Company.

The next doHow® Session is all about comprehensive goal setting, with Drona asking the Contact Manufacturing Team to describe their reality in each of the domains like Response, Kaizen, Morale, Productivity, Profitability/Cashflow, Delivery, Quality, etc., and the team explaining their perception of the reality. Drona, while noting down their replies also looks at cues from their body language to assess if their sentiments were positive, neutral, or negative, so that the goals can be set for the most critical ones. At the end of the session, as Drona shares the comprehensive goal-setting report, everyone is already thinking of the necessary strategies. Arjun gets another task to get everyone to list out the strategies ahead of the next virtual doHow® session. Drona suggests some routines, especially on the areas which had each of the team making different choices.

Drona just walks in five minutes ahead of the next doHow® session to see everyone except Heinrich already present. As

Heinrich rushes in just in time to tell everyone that he was taking a printout of the strategies he has identified, Drona connects his laptop to the projector and logs in to the doHow® Performance Excellence Platform and starts explaining the individual and collective tasks for inspirational persuasion, before creating two groups. They continue with the individual and collective tasks as they keep identifying the macro strategies. After about ninety min, Drona concludes the individual and collective tasks with a short feedback from everyone and opens the doHow® session report to note down the strategies identified during the individual and collective tasks. Now, Drona introduces the CORE and sets up the basics to start with the CORE immediately. It is already two hours and thirty minutes, and he senses everyone being impatient and assures completion before within the planned three hours as he details the supply chain strategy for one expectation of on-time-in-full delivery caused by the fragile/scarce resource materials, impacting the customer for deliveries and shareholders for turnover. He then gets back to the doHow® session report as he defines the homework of detailing the strategy to everyone. The team gets further clarity on the extremely structured doHow® Performance Excellence Platform, as they leave inspired for their lunch.

Tadashi is the first to start detailing his strategies. He plans four strategies. Heinrich defines six strategies, Arjun two, Mohammed five, Geetha three, Naomi four and Julio seven. Since the definitions are done anonymously, no one knows who the strategy owner is, as each of them reviews the already-defined ones before adding theirs. This makes the strategy development comprehensive, covering diverse perspectives, the proven key to successful strategy development. Everyone now sees why they weren't effective when each of them was contributing by stretching themselves beyond limits. The strategy detailing report in the doHow® APP is such an eye opener that each of them starts becoming effective, and Julio is really pleased to see the improving results.

Mohammed comes under pressure as the order pipeline slowly reduces, and he must not only acquire new orders but also start working on their diversification plans as capacity keeps getting released with continual improvements. Mohammed deploys the doHow® APP to his entire team for the driver metrics in sales. While they have already started reaping the benefits from the doHow® Performance Excellence Platform, they eagerly await the next doHow® session.

Drona speaks to Arjun about organising the next doHow® session with the strategy detailing report. Arjun explains that they are all already in sync with each of the strategies and a consensus workshop would not be necessary. He suggests taking the next step instead. Drona is overjoyed at the outcome delivered by the doHow® Performance Excellence Platform and agrees to move to the next phase of doHow® for expanding beyond the core team. He mentions that to do that, they first need to prepare a KPI tree for the detailed strategies, prepare a rolling plan for the KPIs, define the full-kit requirements, and work on process mapping. Together they decide to plan a Teams call with the entire team as the next doHow® session to discuss the next activities towards sustainable profitable growth.

Drona is again surprised that everyone has logged in to the Teams call by the time he logs in three minutes ahead of 10:00. They are all anxious to discover the next steps of their doHow® Performance Excellence Platform journey. Drona first opens the strategy detailing report after sharing his screen for any discussions. He is surprised and inspired by the unanimous agreement on the strategies detailed by all. He introduces the concept of the rolling plan and targets to them and recommends the owners for defining the rolling plan templates, with the metrics to be considered: Julio for the Yearly Business Plan, Mohammed for the Quarterly P&L Plan, Naomi for the Monthly Resources Plan, Tadashi along with Geetha for the Weekly Operation Drivers Plan, and Heinrich along with Arjun for the Daily Delivery Plan. The team agrees to his suggestions. Drona then opens the rolling plan template module and explains what needs to be done. He also explains the concept of yearly, quarterly, monthly, weekly, and daily rolling plans and the three possible KPI hierarchies: a narrower time zone, a driver or lead metric, or drilling down as the possible options. He also explains the KPI directory, which can be used as a guide. Finally, Drona opens the doHow® session report and documents the content of the session along with the actions for preparing the rolling plan templates. At the end of the doHow® session, almost everyone has something to say about the structured flow of the doHow® Performance Excellence Platform, starting from the Stakeholder Expectations to defining the rolling plans and the targets for deployment. They now see even more clearly the light at the end of the tunnel for delighting their stakeholders. They sign off on an extremely positive and promising note.

Drona checks with Arjun on the progress each has made in preparing the rolling plan templates. He is pleased as Arjun shares his screen to show the templates in the doHow® Performance Excellence Platform. Drona makes some suggestions on minor changes so that Arjun can coordinate ahead of the next doHow® session. He also suggests checking if anyone can facilitate the next doHow® session, mainly discussing the rolling plan templates. Arjun volunteers to facilitate.

Arjun speaks to each of his colleagues about Drona's suggestions on the rolling plan template. In his role as the facilitator, Arjun logs in fifteen minutes ahead of schedule and starts sharing his screen with the yearly business plan template. Once everyone joins, they discuss and make some minor changes right then and there. After completing the rolling plan discussion, Arjun passes on the facilitation to Drona. Drona is pleased with the ongoing discussions and now introduces the rolling plan, which needs to be done as per the templates developed. He suggests that the planning sequence must be yearly, quarterly, monthly, weekly, and daily. Heinrich mentions that they already have all the data for the planning, though in different formats. He finds the rolling plan interesting and volunteers to prepare all the plans with the available data so that the owners recommended by Drona can review them by the next doHow® session.

There is unanimous agreement to his suggestion. Drona ends the doHow® session with the normal report.

Drona checks out the rolling plans created by each of them for the year, quarter, month, week, and day. He is pleased with the understanding of each of the rolling plan owners and reaches the Contract Manufacturing Company on time for the next face-to-face doHow® session.

As usual, everyone enters the conference hall on time as Drona is waiting with the projector connected. After a brief introduction by Julio, Drona scrolls down all the rolling plans. He notices that the rolling plans have been done with a good amount of stretch. Based on Drona's suggestion to keep the Estimate (0 Time Zone) and Plan (+1 Time Zone) as realistic as possible, add a slight stretch to the Forecast (+2 Time Zone), and add a challenging stretch to the Target (+3 Time Zone), the rolling plan owners quickly edit their respective rolling plans for the next step. It is already 11:30 by the time the rolling plans are updated and signed off by everyone. At this point, Drona introduces the Execution Planning, a module to be used for the Estimate (0 Time Zone) of the quarterly plan to start with, and then in future to be used at the end of each quarter for the next quarter plan (+1 Time Zone). He additionally explains the options to create a process map or a full-kit template as additional support for reliably fulfilling the targets. He ends the doHow® session with a report, as usual, after defining the homework for each of them to prepare their own execution planning, including the definition of one-time actions and recurring routines to be performed by their colleagues. The Contract Manufacturing Company team gains further clarity on how doHow® brings in clarity on what needs to be done, by whom, and when, for fulfilling the rolling plans.

Drona suggests the agenda for the next doHow® session, where each of them will get about fifteen minutes to present their execution plans for discussion. He also suggests continuing the weekly and daily rolling planning as a standard activity.

Heinrich, the meticulous planner, is extremely impressed with the planning granularity that doHow® has created for the Contract Manufacturing Company.

Tadashi is convinced that their dream of consistently delivering on time in full with zero defects will soon be a reality.

Before departing, they discuss that doHow® is not merely a training programme but a way of working efficiently for effectiveness.

Drona suggests to Arjun to plan the next doHow® session as a virtual one since it will involve presentations by each of them. In line with the suggestion, Arjun updates all the participants.

On Thursday at 10:00, after everyone promptly logs in to the Teams call, Drona suggests an alphabetical order for the execution plan presentations, with Arjun going first, followed by Heinrich, Julio, Mohammed, Naomi, Geetha, and finally Tadashi.

Drona knows that this individual execution plan presentation is the core of creating ownership for the outcomes. He attentively listens to the presentations with some suggestions to make the plan more grounded and focused. Once the presentations are done, Drona mentions that the Contract Manufacturing Company is now ready to play the success game, with everyone reporting their contributions on a daily basis. He shows how Naomi's report looks as an example and how much time it takes. He cautions not to go to the next level until all of them are comfortable.

He also shows the review module and suggests starting to use this module for their daily meetings.

Now that the success game has started, Drona suggests just discussing the performance scoreboard and the fulfilment tracker in the next three doHow® sessions before going to the next step. He also offers 24x7 email support for any queries they may have during the execution phase.

During the next three doHow® sessions, as planned, they discuss the fulfilment tracker and the performance scoreboard. After every presentation, Drona keeps insisting on the learning, both with favourable and adverse effects. He also mentions that progress in any company can be faster with shorter and quicker learning loops, for which the rolling plan is needed at different clockspeeds.

During the last doHow® session, Drona introduces the Debriefing with AAR module, precisely for this learning. As he enters the debriefing for Naomi, he explains that doHow® is an efficient way of working for effectiveness, which can only be learnt with practice and therefore insists on everyone filling up at least three debriefing topics. He ends the last doHow® session with a proposed agenda of brainstorming and problem-solving for the next session.

Julio suggests focusing on productivity for the next problem-solving doHow® session. By now, everyone is not only used to the doHow® Performance Excellence Platform modules introduced by Drona but also comfortable with the other analysing and thinking modules.

When they meet up on Thursday, Julio opens the fulfilment tracker for productivity and explains the gap. The bar graph showing the productivity of different components reveals that the bottom flange has the least productivity. Productivity, being the rate of change in the value added per person, allows for a like-to-like comparison across products. They see that the bottom flange productivity is about 1% compared to over 6% in other products, making it the top contributor to the issue.

Drona acknowledges their observation and reinforces the importance of focusing on one contributor at a time, particularly the worst metric, for faster progress. The principle of "Less is more", or the Pareto principle is well-known and common sense.

Now that they have narrowed down to the bottom flange, they split into two teams and head to the shop floor to fill up the VSM module. This guided module helps them look for opportunities to improve the flow and, hence, productivity. By the time both teams return, they have identified at least twelve new opportunities.

Drona insists that these opportunities be implemented within a week, so that during the next doHow® session, they can observe the changes in productivity. The team sees the benefit of focusing on fewer issues and agrees to complete the actions.

With Arjun now comfortable with the doHow® Performance Excellence Platform, he prepares the doHow® session report. The performance scoreboard with the ranking of all the employees of the Contract Manufacturing Company in the doHow® Performance Excellence Platform becomes a standard and the job at Contract Manufacturing Company becomes more like sports with every employee wanting to climb up in the performance rank through better, smarter working with efficiency as well as effectiveness.

The Contract Manufacturing Company can now SUSTAIN their performance to ADVANCE again after a short period of SUSTAIN to fully internalise the newly acquired wisdom. During this entire duration, Arjun gets visible and recognised for his contribution in transforming the team and the potential he has. Geetha, after a thorough analysis, happily admits Arjun to their top talent pool for an accelerated career. Arjun eventually becomes a role model for the age-old proverb 'A small seed can grow into a mighty tree' with him being proactive to seek a solution to his work/life balance.

Conclusion

Embarking on the journey of the Prosperity doHow® is akin to revisiting the timeless wisdom captured in Dinakar Murthy Krishna's transformative guide. As you reflect on the insights gleaned from its pages, remember the moments of clarity, the sparks of inspiration, and the profound realisations that each chapter offered. The Prosperity doHow® is not just a methodology; it is a beacon of hope and a roadmap to a brighter, more prosperous future.

CORE: Establishing a Strong Foundation

The CORE practice, which stands for Common Understanding, Ongoing Pledge, Regular Audit, and Endless Retraining, sets a solid foundation for your journey. Reflect on the times when aligning with your organisation's mission, vision, and values brought about a sense of unity and purpose. Remember the power of daily pledges and regular audits in reinforcing discipline and excellence. These moments of shared understanding and commitment are the bedrock upon which all future successes are built.

SUSTAIN: Building Resilience and Consistency

SUSTAIN takes the principles of CORE and weaves them into the fabric of your organisation's strategy and operations. As you reminisce about the times when strategic initiatives were seamlessly implemented and consistently monitored, you can appreciate the strength and resilience this practice brings. Think of the collaborative efforts, the detailed execution plans, and the regular dialogues that ensured your organisation stayed on course, continuously adapting and improving. These memories are a testament to the enduring power of collective effort and strategic alignment.

ADVANCE: Driving Continuous Improvement and Innovation

ADVANCE represents the phases of growth and transformation that propel your organisation forward. Recall the excitement of setting detailed goals, the challenge of overcoming resistance, and the satisfaction of nurturing continuous learning. Remember how addressing confusion and consolidating new learning led to establishing a new, improved status quo. These phases are more than just steps; they are the lifeblood of innovation and progress, ensuring that your organisation is always moving forward, always evolving.

Holistic Integration for Success

The Prosperity doHow® also emphasises integrative practices such as stakeholder analysis, 360° goal setting, and inspirational persuasion. Think back to the times when engaging with stakeholders brought new insights, when setting comprehensive goals aligned everyone towards a common purpose, and when inspirational persuasion ignited a collective drive for excellence. These practices create a cohesive, motivated, and engaged workforce, aligning every aspect of your business towards shared objectives.

Unlocking Potential for Personal and Organisational Growth

The true magic of the Prosperity doHow® lies in its ability to unlock the potential within each individual and organisation. Remember the moments of personal growth and increased competence, the times when achieving excellence brought profound happiness and fulfilment. By internalising these principles, you can transform not only your organisation but also your own life, achieving a higher quality of existence marked by prosperity and joy.

Embracing the Future with Confidence

Imagine a parched horse, eager for the refreshing taste of water, driven by its own thirst to find the nearest stream. This is the essence of the Prosperity doHow® principle: rather than pushing people to simply follow steps, we inspire a deep, intrinsic desire for growth and excellence. By creating an environment where curiosity flourishes, and personal aspirations are nurtured, individuals become naturally driven to seek out innovation and improvement. It's about kindling that inner fire, making the journey towards excellence a passionate quest fuelled by their own thirst for success and mastery.

As you implement the Prosperity doHow®, let the memories of past successes and the insights gained guide you. Embrace the future with confidence, knowing that the principles of CORE, SUSTAIN, and ADVANCE are your trusted companions on this journey. Together, we can build a future where excellence, growth, and happiness are not just dreams but realities that define our everyday lives.

The Prosperity doHow® invites you to reflect, to learn, and to grow. It is a call to remember the lessons of the past and to use them as a foundation for a brighter, more prosperous future. Let these reflections inspire you, let the emotional resonance of your journey fuel your drive, and let the promise of prosperity guide you forward.

References

Books:

Airport, Novel by Arthur Hailey

Hotel, Novel by Arthur Hailey

The Final Diagnosis, Book by Arthur Hailey

The Moneychangers, Novel by Arthur Hailey

Wheels, Novel by Arthur Hailey

In Search of Excellence, Book by Robert H. Waterman Jr. and Tom Peters

The Machine That Changed the World, Book by Daniel Roos, Daniel T. Jones, and James P. Womack

The 7 Habits of Highly Effective People, Book by Stephen Covey

Toyota Way, Book by Jeffrey Liker

The Goal, Novel by Eliyahu M. Goldratt

Necessary But Not Sufficient, Novel by Eliyahu M. Goldratt

It's Not Luck, Novel by Eliyahu M. Goldratt

Critical Chain, Novel by Eliyahu M. Goldratt

Emotional Intelligence, Book by Daniel Goleman

Quiet Leadership: Six Steps to Transforming Performance at Work, Book by David Rock

Your Brain at Work, Book by David Rock

Beyond the Goal: Eliyahu Goldratt Speaks on the Theory of Constraints, Book by Eliyahu M. Goldratt

The Choice, Book by Eliyahu M. Goldratt

Primal Leadership, Book by Daniel Goleman

Autobiography of a Yogi, Book by Paramahansa Yogananda

The Necessary Revolution: Working Together to Create a Sustainable World, Book by Peter Senge, Bryan Smith, Nina Kruschwitz, Joe Laur and Sara Schley

Dianetics: The Modern Science of Mental Health, Book by L. Ron Hubbard

The DaVinci Method, Book by Garret John LoPorto

The 8th Habit, Book by Stephen Covey

The Power of Habit, Book by Charles Duhigg

Blue Ocean Strategy, Book by Renée Mauborgne and W. Chan Kim

Type Talk at Work: How the 16 Personality Types Determine Your Success on the Job, Book by Otto Kroeger, Janet M. Thuesen, Hile Rutledge

The Sandler Rules: Forty-Nine Timeless Selling Principles. and How to Apply Them, Book by David Mattson

The Agile Mindset: Developing Employees, Shaping the Future of Work, Book by Svenja Hofert

Great by Choice, Book by James C. Collins

Spiral Dynamics Integral, Book by Don Beck

Websites/Weblinks:

Socratic Method: https://en.wikipedia.org/wiki/Socratic_method

PDCA: https://en.wikipedia.org/wiki/PDCA

Hoshin Kanri: https://en.wikipedia.org/wiki/Hoshin_Kanri

HBR Article – Decoding the DNA of Toyota Production System: https://hbr.org/1999/09/decoding-the-dna-of-the-toyota-production-system

Bereitsschaftspotential: https://en.wikipedia.org/wiki/Bereitschaftspotential

Libet Experiment: https://en.wikipedia.org/wiki/Benjamin_Libet

Kübler Ross Change Curve: https://en.wikipedia.org/wiki/Five_stages_of_grief

EFQM Model: https://efqm.org/the-efqm-model/

CMMI: https://en.wikipedia.org/wiki/Capability_Maturity_Model_Integration

ZED: https://zed.msme.gov.in/objective

KPI: https://en.wikipedia.org/wiki/Performance_indicator

ERA: https://de.wikipedia.org/wiki/Entgelt-Rahmenabkommen

Mercer IPE: https://www.mercer.com/solutions/talent-and-rewards/job-architecture/job-evaluation-ipe/

NSDC QP-NOS: https://nsdcindia.org/nos

Insights Discovery: https://www.insights.com/products/insights-discovery/

Enneagram: https://en.wikipedia.org/wiki/Enneagram_of_Personality

MBTI: https://en.wikipedia.org/wiki/Myers%E2%80%93Briggs_Type_Indicator

CCPM: https://en.wikipedia.org/wiki/Critical_chain_project_management

Seven Quality Tools: https://en.wikipedia.org/wiki/Seven_basic_tools_of_quality